inspired

THE IDEAS THAT SHAPE & CREATE MY DESIGN

JAMIE DURIE

inspired

THE IDEAS THAT SHAPE & CREATE MY DESIGN

JAMIE DURIE

This book is dedicated to my friend, architect Walter Barda, whose work is a constant inspiration to me... thank you for helping me build my dream.

PUBLISHED BY JAMIE DURIE PUBLISHING

JPD MEDIA PTY LTD
ABN 83 098 894 761
35 Albany Street
Crows Nest NSW 2065
PHONE: + 61 2 9026 7444
FAX: + 61 2 9026 7475

FOUNDER AND EDITORIAL DIRECTOR: Jamie Durie
GROUP CREATIVE DIRECTOR: Nadine Bush

PUBLISHER: Nicola Hartley
MANAGING EDITOR: Bettina Hodgson
DESIGN CONCEPT AND ART DIRECTION: Amanda Emmerson
DESIGN: Amanda Emmerson, Anthony Battaglia
and Criena Court
PUBLISHING SERVICES MANAGER: Belinda Smithyman
PUBLISHING ASSISTANT: Michelle Kavanagh
PROJECT EDITORS: Heidi Dokulil and Peter Salhani
TECHNICAL EDITOR: Sebastian Tesoriero
PROOFREADER: Susin Chow
PRINCIPAL PHOTOGRAPHER: Simon Kenny
TRAVEL PHOTOGRAPHY: Jamie Durie
ADDITIONAL PHOTOGRAPHY: Jason Busch, David James,
Georgie Cole, Georgia Moxham and Jerry Harpur
STYLING: Nadine Bush and Jo Carmichael
CONCEPT ILLUSTRATIONS: Alex Augustyn
GARDEN PLANS: PATIO Landscape Architecture and Design

DISTRIBUTED BY: HarperCollins*Publishers* Australia

National Library of Australia Cataloguing-in-Publication data:
Durie, Jamie
Inspired

ISBN 0 9757361 4 0 (hbk)
1. Gardens – Design. 2. Landscape gardening.
I. Dokulil, Heidi. II. Title.

712.2

Set in Gotham and Mrs Eaves on InDesign
Pre-press in Singapore by Colourscan
Printed in Singapore by Tien Wah Press
First printed in 2006

10 9 8 7 6 5 4 3 2 1

PUBLISHERS WOULD LIKE TO THANK

For use of garden spaces and locations: Jane, Todd and Alice Gamble;
Erica Kelly; Eduard and Adriana Litver; Tim and Anna Pope; Andrew
and Justine Blake; Paul and Kathy Panichi, with construction by
Newscapes Australia Pty Ltd; Colin Mitchell, Michelle Klinger and Molly
Mitchell; Terry Melvin and Dr Laura Brearley; Marcel and Geoff Thomas;
Cathy Quinn and The Children's Hospital at Westmead; Sasha Reid;
Royal Botanical Gardens, Sydney.

Gardens and resorts for travel photography: Hunter Valley Gardens,
Pokolbin, Australia; Lunuganga and the Bawa Trust, Sri Lanka; Kirana
Spa, Ubud, Bali; The Royal Pita Maha, Ubud, Bali; Four Seasons Resort,
Jimbaran Bay, Bali; Begawan Giri, Ubud, Bali; Baba Al Shams, Dubai;
Getty Center, Los Angeles, U.S.A.

For props assistance: Arida, www.arida.com.au; Bay Swiss,
www.bayswiss.com.au; Coco Republic, www.cocorepublic.com.au;
Cotswold Furniture, www.cotswoldfurniture.com.au;
Eden Gardens & Garden Centre, www.edengardens.com.au;
Freedom, www.freedom.com.au; Ici et La, www.icietla.com.au; Il Papiro,
www.ilpapirofirenze.it; Lloyd loom, www.lloydloomlustyclassics.com.au;
Mokum Textiles, www.mokumtextiles.com; Outdoor furniture Specialists,
www.outdoorfurnspec.com.au; Papaya, www.papaya.com.au;
Rivas Design, www.rivasdesign.com.au

For copyright and copyright assitance:
Pages 22–23: Made Wijaya
Pages 66–69: Barragan Foundation, Switzerland/ProLitteris,
Zürich, Switzerland.
Pages 102: Quote from *The Modern Japanese Garden* by
Michiko Rico Nosé, printed with permission by Mitchell Beazley,
an imprint of Octopus Publishing Group Ltd.
Pages 170: Quote from *The Australian Roadside* by Edna Walling,
printed with permission by Edna Walling, La Trobe Australian
Manuscripts Collection, State Library of Victoria.

Special thanks to all the team at PATIO Landscape Architecture
and Design for content assistance.

**If you would like to find out more about Jamie and
PATIO Landscape Architecture and Design, please
visit www.patio.com.au**

OTHER JAMIE DURIE BOOKS

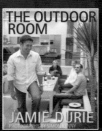

contents

My home...
I like to surround myself
with things that feed my soul
and inspire me. It's then I find
my creativity comes out.

Yunnie

Lush Tropical
33
Hot & Dry
65
Cool Temperate
99
Sensory
131
new directions
165

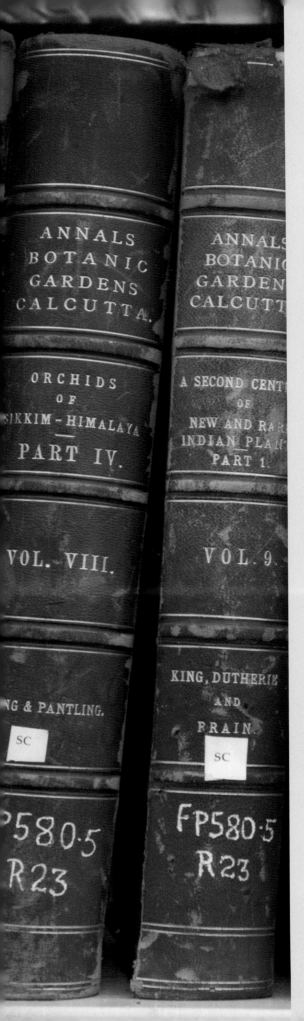

ACKNOWLEDGMENTS

To Geoffrey Bawa, meeting you in person and spending those precious hours together in your garden was an epiphany that will stay with me forever. Your ability to second-guess nature's hand and connect man's architecture with the natural world is unsurpassable. I will attempt to modestly continue your architectural legacy to the best of my ability. Rest in peace... your humble disciple.

To Made Wijaya, I'm not sure what draws me to you more – your incredible vision and beautiful organic architecture, or your wicked mind. Thank you for your friendship and your inspiration.

To Luis Barragán, thank you for your inspirational colour, bold architecture and vision. Although we never met, you taught me to be bold.

To Robert Irwin, as an artist you are without a doubt one of the most inspirational landscape designers of our century, your growing sculptures spark creative conversation around the globe. More power to you, and may we all take your lead.

To Andy Goldsworthy, although I've never met you I'm constantly in awe of your incredible ability to be able to inject art, architecture, sculpture and vision into our natural world. Your work leaves me speechless and constantly reminds me to push the envelope.

To everybody who has generously opened their doors to let our photographers into your private domains – the thanks is not just from me, but from the many readers you've also inspired with your dream.

To Heidi Dokulil and Peter Salhani, thanks for turning all my scattered thoughts into legible poetry, it was a pleasure to work with you both – you helped me to uncover a few dusty insights!

To my old mate Simon Kenny, it never feels like work with you, just a barrage of blokey jokes. Thank you for your professionalism and your fantastic eye.

To Alex Augustyn, it was so nice to come back to my roots and have your incredibly intuitive hands sculpt my vision on the tiny point of a pencil. Thank you for your insightful interpretation and attention to detail.

To Anthony Battaglia, I look forward to using more of your raw talent in more of our books, thank you.

To Robert Gorman, Jim Demetriou, Robyn Fritchley, Cristina Lee, Emma Lindsay and all of the wonderful staff at HarperCollins*Publishers*, thank you for believing in us and I look forward to many more projects together.

To my Patio and JPD Media extended family – in particular Stephen Wells, Jenny Wheatley, Dejana Milinkovic and Julian Brady – where would I be without you? Thank you for your inspiring skill and creativity.

Nadine Bush – thank you so much for your incredible devotion, not just to this project, but to everything you touch. Once again you have kept my creative flame alight, and your ideas are not only invaluable but they exude warmth and a feeling of freshness that we all strive for. I couldn't have pulled this off without you my love – it never feels like work. Love Jamie.

Nicci Hartley – thank you so much for instigating and encouraging me to create this book, for your incredible patience and for turning my unorthodox ideas into strong palatable publishing concepts. Your ability to produce top quality work with amazing attention to detail and compounding deadlines is astounding.

Bettina Hodgson – your intuition and ability to rise above any obstacles in your way is inspiring. Thank you for all of your hard work, stylish intuition, and your determination and constant quest for perfection.

Amanda Emmerson – thank you for all your fantastic insight and your wonderful creativity, not to mention the late nights to make it all happen. Your visual poetry has made us all very proud of this project.

Belinda Smithyman – I can't thank you enough for your loyalty, your laughs and your undying enthusiasm. Good luck with the 'bump' – we will be thinking of you.

Criena Court – your raw creativity has been a breath of fresh air, thank you so much for your valuable input and I'm looking forward to working with you on many more projects.

Michelle Kavanagh – thanks for taking the leap, it is obvious you can apply yourself to just about any role within our family, and you do it with pride and diligence... nice one!

Sebastian Tesoriero – once again our horticultural hero saves the day! Where would we be with out you? Probably floundering in botanical illiteracy. Thank you for all your incredible attention to detail and your unvarying professional principles.

Giselle Barron and Harriette Rowe – thank you for representing our design office with such grace and style. The PATIO drawings and your contributions to content have given this project enormous credibility. The work fills me with pride.

Thank you to my friends and family for putting up with me, and most importantly, to our readers – thank you for your support and loyalty, it means the world to us! We'd love your feedback: www.patio.com.au

'Travel has been my greatest teacher and friend, probably all my life... whether we realise it or not, we always refer to our own personal "hard-drive" of sensory experience.'

Yumi

Earlier this year, I started sorting through my travel snaps. Years' worth of holidays and work trips were collected in boxes and on CDs with thousands of images uncatalogued. I'm the first to admit that organisational skills are not my strong point, which is why I surround myself with a strong team. As I went through the photographs, I began to revisit in my mind some of the wonderful moments and extraordinary places I have been lucky enough to experience. It made me glad I always carry my camera.

In among the photos are, of course, people I have travelled with or met along the way, those who have shared with me their knowledge, wisdom, love and laughter. But there is also enormous variety in scenes and landscapes, patterns and plants that form my working diary of ideas. Staring back at me in the lush, vibrant images of Bali and Sri Lanka, the red rock cliffs and giant cacti in Spain, temples in Japan and African skies was a revelation. Travel has been my greatest teacher and friend, probably all my life.

For me, there has never been a substitute for going there and seeing it in the flesh. Experiencing other cultures and other vistas changes you

immeasurably and intangibly. As I tried to bring some order to the images mounting up in boxes on the bookshelves, I thought a visual record might be a good way to keep track of some of the experiences that have profoundly influenced my life and my work. Hence the idea behind *Inspired*.

In my earlier books – *Patio*, *The Outdoor Room* and *The Source Book*, I was determined to put down in print as many hands-on design tips and ideas as I could. If you're lucky enough to work in your field of passion, I think you've got to share it. To that end, *Inspired* features some of our favourite design projects that have kept myself and the PATIO team busy of late, but this book is different in that it's less about 'how' we build a landscape and more about 'why' we design things in a certain way. In this sense, this is more a scrapbook of ideas, people and places that have inspired me over the years and how these inspirations have been translated into tangible designs.

If it sounds like I've got too much time on my hands, the reverse is actually true. I'm always on the move and I can't imagine slowing down any time soon. I'm too hungry for new experiences and the more I see, the hungrier I grow. But while I'm not the type to look back in life, I think you reach a point where you want to put down roots, and observing the past can help make sense of the future. Putting together these experiences, collected like passport stamps along my travels, has actually helped me reconnect with my design roots and I realise that I'm drawn to extremes. I'm a water baby and I've loved tropical landscapes ever since my first tropical holiday, so chapter one is devoted to this.

When I first opened PATIO, it was a little shop in Sydney. I used to bring back decorative stone bowls, statues and tiles from all over the world which people loved using in their gardens because each piece had a story and sense of age to it. I gathered symbols of other cultures partly because I'd never really found my own, until a few years ago when I made the pilgrimage to Sri Lanka, the birthplace of my mother. That altered my course in life. It was also in Sri Lanka that I met my mentor, the late architect Geoffrey Bawa – the pioneer of what I call the outdoor room. For Bawa, architecture and landscape was one and the same thing. He was the master at creating segues between the indoors and out, and of creating buildings that embrace natural topography and viewpoints of interest.

When we met at Lunuganga, his home of 50 years, he'd suffered a stroke and couldn't speak, but he held my hand for hours while we toured the extraordinary landscape he had sculpted beside a forest a few miles from the coast. This was the greatest design lesson of my life, yet not a word was spoken. Lunuganga is the most inspiring garden fantasy of forests and lakes and little pavilions with just dense green jungle for walls. That's when I became

completely passionate about building gardens for living in – 'human gardens' – and I dedicated my second book, *The Outdoor Room,* to the memory of Geoffrey Bawa, who died nine months after our meeting.

I also love the drama of the desert in Australia and America's southwest, as well as Mexico and Africa, and chapter two looks at these influences. When I first started in show business, I lived in Las Vegas, Nevada, and I felt as much at home in the desert there as I did growing up in the Pilbara as a boy. Dad had worked the Hamersley mine and we lived in the town of Tom Price. It's Australia's richest iron ore belt and one of the most dramatic landscapes in the world where extreme contrasts sit together like scenes from science fiction – from the jagged red mountains of the Hamersley Ranges to the gorges and lush waterholes of Karijini National Park. The scorching summers defeat almost all living things here – though ghost gums, river reds and the Sturt desert pea survive. When the rains come, the ground turns to a thick sea of red mud. This is not a landscape for the faint-hearted, but it's the one I grew up in and I still find such harsh environments thrilling.

Chapter three looks east, to the cool climate and culture of Japan. I went there for the first time in 2003, when PATIO entered its award-winning Contemporary Australian Courtyard in the Pacific Flora World Garden Competition, held in Hamamatsu, Shizuoka prefecture. I loved the pace and edginess of Tokyo, one of the great modern metropolises, but it was the refined temple gardens of Kyoto that seduced me with the simplicity and power of Japanese design philosophy. While my tropical adventures inspired me to make rooms in the garden and take the inside

out, in Japan the role is reversed and gardens tend to bring the outdoors in. They are surely the masters at replicating a huge landscape on a tiny scale, designing gardens like paintings – to be enjoyed from inside the house – perfectly framed in front of a window. Perhaps that's a function of their cooler climate, but its success is also a function of discipline – paring back the ingredients to five essential elements: stone, wood, plants, water and respectful ornamentation. I never fully appreciated simplicity and discipline until I sat in a tiny tea house and looked out at the moss-covered rocks for several hours one wet afternoon. For the first time I understood what 'less is more' really means and it made me want to edit much more carefully the elements I include in my designs.

Chapter four looks at gardens that appeal to our senses on a level beyond the purely visual and in particular the improbable garden at the Getty Center in Los Angeles, designed by American artist Robert Irwin. As designers our job is to manage the mechanics of a landscape so that it works, while an artist brings a different vision with an element of magic. I'm always looking out for new artists working with landscapes because their processes of exploration are to me as inspirational as their finished works, and in this chapter I've shared some of the work that has inspired me.

Chapter five, New Directions, puts into perspective the unique language of landscape design emerging in Australia today. It's about thinking along sustainable lines and caring for the environment. I'm also talking about my own new direction. At the moment I'm on a very personal journey, much closer to home – I'm about to build my first house. All those images and ideas gathered over the years are finally taking shape on the drawing board and my architect, Walter Barda, has generously allowed us to show some of the sketches. Over the years I've helped a lot of people build their own little patch of paradise and I'm often asked what I would do if I were in their shoes. Now, for the first time, I am in their shoes, and I finally have the answer, so I want to share some of it. By the time *Inspired* goes to print, we hope to have begun building, or at least clearing the site, which is a pretty exciting step – a place of my own at last.

Earlier I said that travel has been my teacher, and that's true, but I don't think you have to travel to find design inspiration in nature – it's everywhere. From the patterns made by shadows and light to the veins of a leaf, or even a striking sunset, we need only open our eyes. While on safari in Africa a few years ago, I saw an amazing light show in the sky. At dusk, the sky and clouds had formed into dozens of shades of pinks and apricots, reds, deep magenta and black. I'll never forget it. It seemed everywhere I looked were acacia trees – leafless and sculptural with their lateral branches pinned to the horizon line in silhouette. The glowing sky behind them made me focus on the beauty of these skeletal trees. Nature can leave you speechless sometimes if you let it. I think we underestimate how many pictures our minds can store, and how strongly we hold onto these sights and experiences that move us. Whether we realise it or not, we are always refering to our personal 'hard-drive' of sensory experience. Between the pages of *Inspired* are a few of the experiences that feed me as a designer. I sincerely hope they inspire you too.

Lush Tropical

Sri Lanka

★ National capital

— Province boundary

WESTERN

SABARAGAMUWA

SOUTHERN

SPONSORS. WE DO APPRECIAT YOUR HELP.
FOR THOSE WHO WISH TO SEE THE BIG BUDDHA
TEMPLE DEVELOP OR TO CONTRIBUTE FOR THE
BUDDHA FUND USED PARTICULARLY FOR THE
RESTORATION AND EQUIPMENT, THEY ARE
TO DO FOR HAPPINESS, GOOD HEALTH,
LONGIVITY.

The Royal Pita Maha
A Tjampuhan Relaxation Reso

Desa Kedewatan - P.O.
Tel : 62. 361. 98
e-mail : theroyal@indosat.net.id

KiRANA SPA

Division Manager
Marketing & PR

Made Sum

PT.Pr
Des
naspa.com
tirn.net.id
iranaspa.com

Kirana Spa's beautiful outdoor room

Fabric and stone go hand in hand

The house touches the water which touches the garden

Tropical colour

You can see why they call this a welcome palm

A young monk in training, Sri Lanka

My tropical home away from home

WHEN YOU THINK TROPICAL YOU THINK HOLIDAYS.
TURQUOISE SEA AND LUSH GREEN FOREST, SUNNY DAYS
AND BALMY NIGHTS, REST AND RECREATION. PEOPLE
ALL OVER THE WORLD FLOCK TO THE TROPICS TO BE
ENVELOPED BY NATURE AND RESTORED.

Because the climate is so amazingly perfect, you live outside all the time and the architecture reflects this in homes that are open to the elements with big verandahs jutting into jungles or overlooking the ocean. Perhaps that's why I lean towards tropical landscapes – not just because they are where my heart lies, but because to me they're the most inviting and relaxing.

While there are many places in the tropical world I have visited, and many more still I would like to, it is Bali and Sri Lanka that have had lasting inspiration in my life and my work.

I first visited Bali, 'Island of the Gods', in 1990 when I was just 17. It was my first trip out of Australia and it's fair to say I fell in love with the place. In those days it was a playground for Australians and for many, our first taste of exotica. It certainly was for me.

Bali is a small, highly fertile volcanic island, in the Indonesian archipelago, east of Java and eight degrees south of the equator. Temperatures range from 20 to 33 degrees Celsius every day and from December to March, the monsoon brings heavy rain. The island is draped in lush mountain forests cut by fast-flowing rivers and terraced rice fields. My first impressions were that everything seemed to grow so quickly and effortlessly, you really felt like you were in God's playground. Not only that, the way people lived in their environment was worlds apart from life in Australia even though it was just a few hours away by plane.

Here were beautiful private courtyard-style gardens with their open pavilions furnished decadently with day beds and floor cushions. The pavilions were made from raw, earthy materials – thick carved timbers, thatched roofs and natural stone. I was captivated too by the tropical plants – hibiscus, heliconias, water lilies, jasmine and orchids – all huge and growing prolifically. Magnolia and frangipani trees flourishing like I'd never seen them in Australia. Lotus flowers (PATIO's motif) the size of saucers floating above lily pads as large as dinner plates.

That's the beauty of the tropics; they're all about abundance. And water. Water is what defines and carves the landscape. I felt this powerfully in the mountains of Ubud – Bali's artistic hub. It's so steep, so lush. Water is either raging in a river torrent, or lying tranquil in a terraced rice field. I love what water brings to a landscape. As a designer, I'm always looking for ways to capture some of those moods – serenity, excitement, colour and movement – and water features have become one of my favourite elements to design.

In Ubud, I visited the then-named Begawan Giri – perhaps the most beautiful hotel resort I've ever seen. This resort is pure indulgence, but also what the tropics are about. Set among five hectares of rainforest, it has five stand-out residences, each with a theme – fire, wind, water, forest and earth. Pools of reflective water surround the dining and living pavilion, an open platform with no doors that feels like it's floating. Small islands rise from the water and are planted with frangipanis. A river rages to one side, and beyond a sheer drop, a 20-metre black swimming pool reflects the sky and forest canopy. Adjoining the sleeping pavilion is a giant bathtub carved from a solid piece of basalt. This resort has inspired me ever since my first visit – it's one of the few hotels that has been able to blend luxury and nature so well. Here-in lies the secret to its success.

The tiny island of Sri Lanka off the southeast tip of India, 10 degrees north of the equator, is a steamy botanical hothouse. Daily temperatures average 27 to 29 degrees Celsius and the monsoons soak from May to September and December to

Begawan Giri

February. Lapped by the warm waters of the Indian Ocean, it is known as 'The Spice Island' for its abundance of culinary plants – from pepper and cocoa to its most famous fragrant exports, cardamom, cloves and cinnamon.

Spices brought the traders and the conquerors to Ceylon, as it was once known, and like many ports along the ancient trading routes, the island suffered wave after wave of colonial rule. The Arabs, the Portuguese, the Dutch and the British have all controlled it. Today it still bears that diverse cultural legacy. When the British expelled the Dutch in 1795, they established coffee plantations in the lush central highlands, but these were wiped out a hundred years ago by fungus. Camellia bushes were brought in from India to replace the coffee, and become Sri Lanka's other major export crop – tea.

I ventured to Sri Lanka, birthplace of my mother, only a few years ago. I knew very little about the place or my heritage, so for me it was a pilgrimage. I went with fellow Aussie–Sri Lankan Geoff Janz, and together we traced our roots, took in the sights and made a television special in the process. It was one of the most rewarding journeys for me, not just because I connected with my personal history, but because here I had two experiences that deeply affected my thinking about landscape design.

The first was Sigiriya Rock, the fortified palace and city of King Kasyapa, built on a mountaintop some 1500 years ago and 3200 feet above sea level. With over 80 gravity-fed water features, ponds and fountains, its sheer improbability of scale and engineering blew me away. The way in which water was harnessed in huge rock pools carved by hand, then channelled for drinking, bathing and irrigating the gardens, would challenge even today's technology and designers.

The other uplifting experience for me in Sri Lanka was meeting Geoffrey Bawa, the country's most revered architect, before he died in 2003. He is probably my greatest inspiration and the pioneer of the outdoor living space, what I call the outdoor room, that defines tropical living. We met at his home, Lunuganga. Here are lush secluded gardens and loggias falling into the house. Lounge suites extend from the living rooms out into the courtyard, and resting places scattered throughout the gardens wait to be discovered. The great lesson I learnt from Lunuganga is the impact of level changes to consolidate the focus of a landscape, because it allows you to direct the viewer's attention to the immediate foreground without distraction and to keep other areas hidden for later surprise. This lesson has become one of the greatest design tools on my belt; it is a wonderful way to add drama or intrigue into a plot with uninteresting topography. Bawa made a lot of changes to the ground level – from gentle slopes that blend one area into another, to sheer, steep drops that dramatically highlight vantage points and views. His designs teach to never give away all of the landscape at one glance; applying this lesson gives me the opportunity to provide the gifts of discovery and intrigue in the gardens I create.

GEOFFREY BAWA

GEOFFREY BAWA (1919–2003) was born in Sri Lanka, but spent much of his young life away from Ceylon, as the country was then known, studying English and practising law. He returned in 1948 at the end of British rule and at 38 years of age qualified as a landscape architect, with twin passions for his country's forgotten architecture and the new techniques of construction.

For many, Bawa is a guru of architecture for the tropics and for the senses. He is most remembered for buildings and gardens that forge an intimate link to their landscape with open-sided pavilions combining Western architectural symmetry with Eastern harmony, craftsmanship and love of nature and natural materials.

His first courtyard house in Colombo was designed for Ena de Silva. The site was small and de Silva wanted rooms opening to courtyards, but privacy from the neighbours. Bawa devised an inward-looking house with linked pavilions and courtyards around a central courtyard that was lined with stone and designed to become a river during the rainy season. The house was set on a small site, and is an influential blueprint for the opening up of modern houses to their gardens, or terraces to the light.

Rohan Balasriya Residence

Bawa's home was Lunuganga – an old estate on Sri Lanka's southwest coast in Bentoto, two hours' drive from Colombo, one mile from the coast. Under Dutch rule (1658–1795) it had been a cinnamon garden; under British rule a rubber plantation. When Bawa bought it in 1948, it was in decline, the house swamped by 25 acres of rubber trees, set on the most fertile part of the island around Dedduwa Lake, and fringed to the east by Sinharaja Forest, Sri Lanka's last surviving ancient rainforest.

Over five decades Bawa transformed the property, replanting native woodlands and opening up new vistas. He told me how he used herds of elephants to excavate and lower hills that obstructed important views beyond the lake. I'm still in awe and perhaps a little envious whenever I picture those elephants moving mountains to sculpt his garden vistas. Bawa had a great affinity with nature and was forever bending it to his purpose. In Ena de Silva's Colombo house he shaped a large frangipani tree by hanging sandbags from its lower branches to weigh them down and stretch them, manipulating it to a more romantic form.

Geoffrey Bawa Office – The Gallery

But Bawa was not painting static pictures. At Lunuganga he was sculpting a landscape for people to enjoy. He turned the original house virtually inside out by adding verandahs, courtyards and satellite rooms, extending it always into the garden. He was constantly building pavilions around the property that consisted of little more than a floor and pillars supporting a roof. Often they embodied something of Sri Lanka's traditional building style, but with Bawa's Western-trained eye. For him, they served as models for larger projects, and it's said that his design for the old Parliament House in Kotte was actually inspired by the 'hen house' pavilion at Lunuganga which was elegantly composed of four brick pillars, a tiled roof, three lattice walls and a door.

The pavilions were resting places, destinations to discover along the journey through the garden. Some Bawa used as his own private thinking (or working) places, or as retreats for guests – he hosted all manner of visiting dignitaries at Lunuganga, from royalty to rock stars, as well as devoted disciples like me. He also hosted many people from the creative arts, offering his estate as a retreat, and this legacy continues today with an artists residency program managed by the Bawa Trust. The house itself has recently opened as a guesthouse, available from December to April only, and you can tour the gardens by appointment.

Ena de Silva's House – Artist's Residence

Ena de Silva's House – Artist's Residence

ORCHID ROOM

STONE SLABS

STONE SLAB WALL

STONE PAVEMENT

The concept for this design is straightforward – it is almost like taking the roof off a typical house and furnishing the rooms with plants. A simple design plan that is often under-utilised, it is one that offers intimacy and choice by compartmentalising the garden compound.

Garden design by Jamie Durie. Illustration by Alex Augustyn.

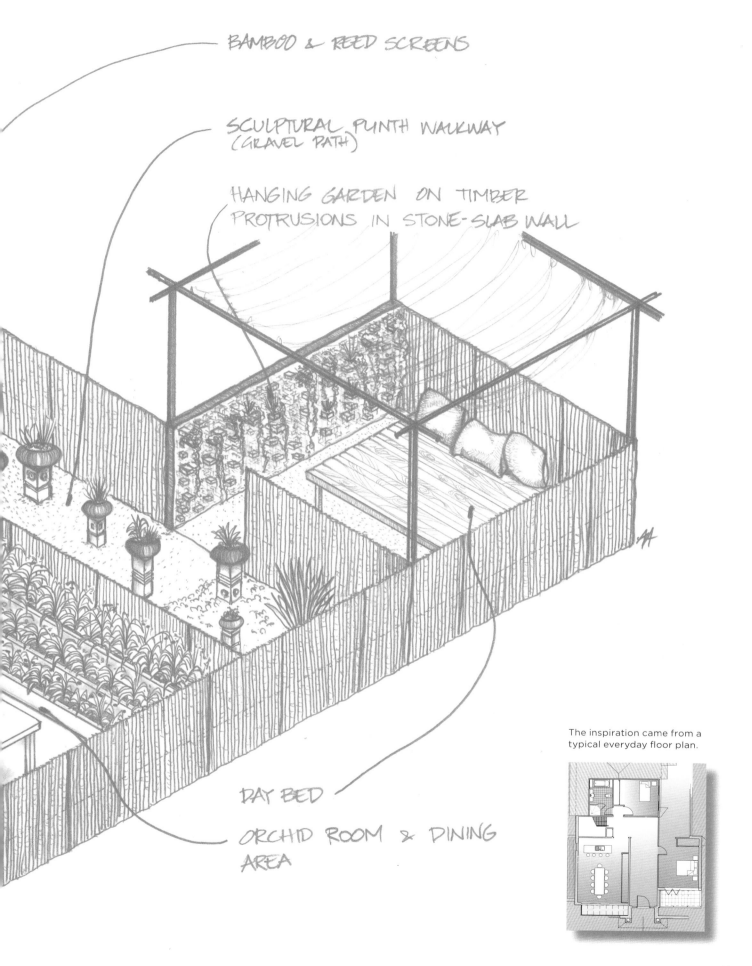

BAMBOO & REED SCREENS

SCULPTURAL PLINTH WALKWAY
(GRAVEL PATH)

HANGING GARDEN ON TIMBER
PROTRUSIONS IN STONE-SLAB WALL

DAY BED

ORCHID ROOM & DINING
AREA

The inspiration came from a
typical everyday floor plan.

MADE WIJAYA

A Jepun pedestal fountain, Villa Bebek

Architect and landscaper MADE WIJAYA is an authority on Balinese architecture, and he influenced a lot of the Bali style that first came to Australia.

Born in Australia as Michael White, he was spellbound on his first visit to Bali in the early 1980s. So much so that he changed his name, moved there almost immediately and has lived there ever since. He's one of few Westerners to completely immerse themselves in Balinese culture and become fluent in the language. Made travelled extensively through Bali and comprehensively recorded its traditional building styles and materials, publishing several books on the subject.

From his early years there, Made loved playing with the palette of tropical plants and colours and the primitive-style carved wood and stone by local artisans. He later developed his own hybrid styles such as 'Tropical Cotswolds', that display a mixture of formal English garden symmetry with the loose and lush plants of the tropics. The gardens he designs are often densely layered with palms, waterlilies, vines and vibrant flowering shrubs laid out using classical geometry.

A passionate visionary with a true love for the Balinese culture, Made's work has taught me to always respect culture and traditional art, craft and architecture. Today he has more than 400 gardens in the tropical world to his credit and his own estate, Villa Bebek, at Sanur is his laboratory. A mentor and friend of mine for some time, Made is also quite a colourful character – not just for the gardens he creates, but the enthusiasm with which he creates them – using a 'commando-style' team of Balinese gardening artisans whose credo is to achieve the maximum impact in 'tropical' time.

Terrace, Villa Bebek

Swimming pool, Villa Bebek

FOREST TRACKS

Brisbane swelters in the summer, but this residential garden had more than its share of shade. A mature poinciana (*Delonix regia*) stretched from the rear of the garden almost to the house, so light was dappled and the ground always damp. One of the owners, a ceramic artist, had her studio at the rear of the house opening out to the garden; however, the garden did not invite them outdoors.

The idea for this garden was to create an inspirational sanctuary, a lush environment to encourage creativity, as well as a usable garden for play outside the house. The owners needed small areas to display sculpture and art, somewhere quiet to sit and play music, and a place for their young daughter to enjoy her own little piece of the garden.

The site was perfect for creating a little rainforest walk linked to the house. A new timber deck extends the studio into the garden and doubles as a dining area. From here, raised timber boardwalks divide the centre of the garden into a grid pattern. With this raised design I wanted the person walking through the garden to feel like they were floating across the foliage. The walkways lead to little destinations or 'end points' where screens of slatted timber woven with rope stand as backdrops for art installations. Large white concrete bowls form focal points along the track and are planted with striking burgundy imperial bromeliads (*Alcantarea imperialis*) that can reach more than 1 metre in the shade.

Beds between the walkways are filled with glossy green-leaved plants – lady palms (*Rhapis excelsa*), peace lilies (*Spathiphyllum*) and *Philodendron* 'Xanadu' – or colourful bromeliads such as *Neoregelia* and *Vriesea*. Some have giant black bamboo (*Bambusa lako*) and buddha belly bamboo (*Bambusa ventricosa*) planted as living screens.

At the base of the poinciana tree, a cubby house on stilts has been built for the kids to have their own spot to enjoy. The nearby clump of upright elephants' ears (*Alocasia portadora*) will eventually obscure it from the house. To one side of the boardwalk is a sunken courtyard area, mapped out with low walls and limestone paving. Furnished simply with a primitive-style carved timber bench, it is a quiet spot for meditation or for just enjoying the view.

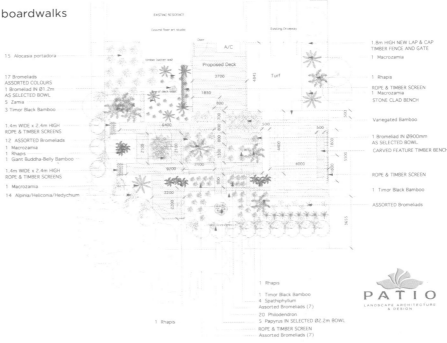

(ABOVE) A secluded seating area is paved with limestone and furnished with an Indonesian carved timber bench. Behind it are screens of timber slats roped together.

(LEFT) The raised boardwalk has planted pockets of bromeliads and other shade lovers, plus black bamboo and lady palms. Concrete pots of varying shapes, planted with imperial bromeliads, present focal points of interest along the track.

(ABOVE) The timber boardwalk zigzags through the garden, encouraging it to be explored from many different angles.

(RIGHT) Timber slatted screens strung together by rope make natural backdrops for artistic displays of potted bromeliads or the owner's ceramic sculptures. Beside the 'cubby/tree house' are upright elephants' ears.

PRIVATE RESORT

The swimming pool and cabana behind this family home had seen better days. The large pool was surrounded by a lush semi-tropical garden, but the area was under-utilised because it lacked warmth, lighting and usable furniture to make it an inviting destination.

Part of the solution was to capitalise on the garden's remoteness from the house, and give the area the feel of a luxurious tropical resort – where the pool is always the best place to be. A warm palette of timber, sandstone and copper now defines the pool area – the perfect natural elements for these lush surrounds.

Timber decking surrounds the pool and in certain spots is cantilevered over the edge as a platform for diving or sunbathing. At the end closest to the house, the deck steps down into the pool with a generous tallowwood ledge to sit on, submerging you waist-deep in the water. At the northern end, the deck curves up onto the wall as a sculptural

screen for privacy from the neighbours. Also enticing people down to this end of the pool area are three timber pontoons stacked beside a wall of greenery. Kentia palms (*Howea forsteriana*) growing through holes cut in the deck extend the greenery forward. It's a secluded place to throw down a towel and catch the sun as it moves around the garden.

At night the pool area comes alive with three light towers of frosted glass casting a warm amber glow over the green pool that's much more flattering and comfortable for entertaining than harsh direct lighting. Timber louvres diffuse the light on the sides while at the front of each tower, light catches water as it flows down the face of the frosted glass, through channels of white pebbles, and gently into the pool. The terraced copper planters at the ground level of the light towers have a lush green carpet of convolvulus (*Convolvulus sabatius* ssp. *mauritanicus*) spilling down to the deck.

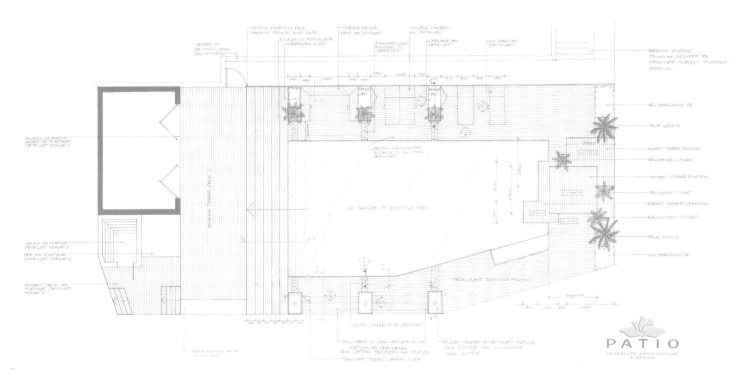

PATIO
LANDSCAPE ARCHITECTURE & DESIGN

FLOATING ON FOLIAGE

This garden is based on the Sri Lankan vernacular housing tradition of channelling pure rainwater off the roof and into internal ponds within landscaped courtyards. The focus of the garden is the precious resource of water that takes the form of a serene reflection pool.

Mass planting for texture and colour fill every corner of the space so that the built elements appear to rise from a lush carpet of foliage. The plant palette is mostly in shades of green and red with timber structures and red slate stepping stones. In front of a feature screen of horizontal stacked timber battens is a striking row of deep burgundy *Cordyline fruticosa* 'Caruba Black' planted densely for a solid mass. The perimeter walls are limewashed in a musk pink for flashes of hot colour behind the foliage. The raised planter beds in front are a more subdued bluestone hue which ties them to the cordylines.

Waterlilies (*Nymphaea*) and lotus (*Nelumbo nucifera*) in the pond break its dark reflective surface with flashes of leaves and flowers, and when the rain brings water off the roof flooding into it, the pond comes to life. A shower within the pond area is fed by rainwater when available and supplemented by heated water, and wastewater is collected below the lattice platform for recycling.

In the tradition of the tropics, the outdoor space is luxuriously furnished. Above the pond and suspended from a pergola of chunky timber beams is a day bed curved in the form of a palm husk to cradle the body. A table for dining rises out of the timber deck, requiring guests to sit on the floor to eat in the informal Eastern tradition.

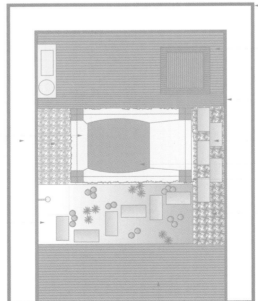

External boundary wall approx 2500mm high constructed of timber frame clad in blue board. The timber frame is made up of 90 x 90mm sections with a bottom plate of these dimensions to distribute the The wall is to be secured to the ground every 2400mm with a star picket maximur 400mm.

Timber deck laid on 90 x 90mm bearers at These bearers are to sit on a 150 x 25mm distribute the load, allowing it to follow any Heights are to be achieved by stumps whic All footings are above ground. The structu surrounding structures for stability.

Internal planter wall approx 800mm high constructed of 90 x 90mm timber fr clad in blue board. A base plate will distribute the load. The external boundary wall and the internal planter wa will be braced together to ensure structu

Stepping stones on a timber sleeper pad to lift them to the required level and distribute the load.

Seat is hung from pergola so has no direct footprint on the ground.

Timber pergola is tied at base with 200 x base plate which will distribute the load ar As this feature will experience lateral load: four footings of 300mm diameter, 500mm

Planting in pots raised to height on bed of mulch

Planting in pots raised to height on bed of mulch

Pond made of butyl membrane supported by timber sleeper sides. All footings above ground. No excavation required. Base raised to level with sand.

PATIO
LANDSCAPE ARCHITECTURE
& DESIGN

Timber deck laid on 90 x 90mm bearers at 1m spacings. These bearers are to sit on a 150 x 25mm sole plate to distibute the load, allowing it to follow any ground undulation. Heights are to be acheved by stumps which will sit on the bearer. All footings are above ground. The structure will be tied into surrounding structures for stability.

(ABOVE) The day bedswing is suspended above masses of *Pieris japonica* 'Variegata' with the New Zealand rock lily (*Arthropodium cirratum*) planted in the foreground.

(RIGHT) Built-in seating for the barbecue area is backed by a planter bed with *Cordyline fruticosa* 'Caruba Black'.

(OPPOSITE) Behind the planter beds, anchored to the hot pink wall, is a screen of stacked recycled timber palings that create a focal point of interest along the track.

An outdoor lounging space with a touch of tropical indulgence and all the mod cons including a contoured day bedswing, dining area and outdoor shower over the pond.

ROOM WITH A VIEW

This Sydney garden belongs to a new home built on the grounds of historic Babworth House at Darling Point. It's a steep site with a number of mature trees from the original estate gardens, including a giant fig and Canary Island date palms, one with a strangler fig taking hold. As well as shading much of the garden, the trees frame a picturesque view of the bay between neighbouring houses.

Although there was a large deck off the living area of the home, the garden was a no-man's land and the owners needed more usable space within it. A pavilion with a built-in day bed was constructed at the furthest point from the house, which not only turned an unused dead space into a destination, but also created more interest in the garden between the two points.

Closed at the back for privacy, the pavilion opens on three sides to take in the garden and harbour views. A meandering timber walkway takes you from the main deck to the pavilion via a lower deck furnished with a built-in bench seat and an outdoor shower.

Under the existing canopy of trees, shade-loving tropical plants were added for foliage variety and colour at both ground level and mid-height. Red-centred bromeliads (*Neoregelia*) and peace lilies (*Spathiphyllum*) flank one side of the boardwalk to the pavilion, while on the other side are pink-fringed *Cordyline fruticosa*, bird's nest ferns (*Asplenium*), cardboard palms (*Zamia furfuracea*), *Philodendron* 'Xanadu' and *Ctenanthe* 'Greystar' – with variegated silvery-green leaves. As a magnet to draw the eye towards the pavilion, the raised bed in front is filled with a mass of the bright green variegated leaves of zebra plants (*Calathea zebrina*), a Brazilian native with foliage that has a luminous quality under dappled light.

Being a remote satellite room, nestled into the garden at the end of a track, the pavilion is probably more Geoffrey Bawa than Bali-inspired. It is a simple unadorned structure of rendered brick pillars, with a shingle roof and timber shutters for screening. Cushions and candles are the only embellishments required for this peaceful alcove, apart from a mosquito net for mid-summer sleep-outs.

2 Trachelospermum Tri
2 Trachelospermum Tri

14.465 WALL

EXISTING ST
TO REMAIN.

5 Molineria

9 Calathea

12 Philoden

21

5 Strelitzia re
7 Asplenium aus
3 Dicksonia ant

6 Strelitzia re

5 Rhapis ex

CLUMP OF EXISTING
BANANA'S TO REMAIN.

3 Dicksonia ant
7 Calathea
5 Stromanthe
9 Molineria

EXISTING CORDYLINE
TO BE RELOCATED.

1 Plumeria

5 Cordyline fru
RELOCATE EXISTING BROMILIADS
5 Strelitzia jun
8 Calathea
5 Gardenia au
3 Cordyline fru
5 Syzygium wilsonii

EXISTING SCREEN PLANTING
TO REMAIN.

4 Cordyline fru

11 Molineria
13 Cordyline ru
13 Ctenanthe

...lathea
...ilodendron X
...enium aus
NG CORDYLINE
MAIN.
...ilodendron X
...a fur
...nanthe
...elitzia jun

9 Philodendron X
19 Lomandra con
15 Liriope EG
8 Dietes bi
4 Strelitzia jun

8 Philodendron X
2 Gardenia aug
10 Liriope EG
EXISTING SCREEN PLANTING
TO REMAIN.
11 Spathiphyllum Sen
RELOCATE EXISTING BROMILIADS

STONE WALL
SEWER INSPECTION PIT
TOP OF SMALL WALL
CONCRETE RETAINING WALL
BANANA CLUMP
BRICK
SINGLE STOREY HOUSE
RENDERED ROOF TILE ROOF
FLOOR LEVEL RL 41.05
BANANA CLUMP
LOW RET. WALL
STAIRS
CONCRETE
LAWN
LAWN
PATH
WALL
STEPS
SANDSTONE
TREE

PATIO
LANDSCAPE ARCHITECTURE & DESIGN

The living area opens to a deck
used daily for eating and for
entertaining. A short walk away
is the new pavilion, creating a
more intimate, sheltered retreat
within the garden. It is a simple
structure designed in the style
of pavilions by Geoffrey Bawa.

LUSH TROPICAL
IN FOCUS

Walls of glossy foliage and lacy, leafy canopies. Water

flowing rapidly over rocks into lily ponds and reflection pools.

Brilliant coloured flowers amongst the green. Tropical pavilions

along a rainforest track. Stone tribal artefacts and natural

materials, hand-crafted and weathered with age.

A place for relaxing and lounging by the pool...

and for long summer days soaking

up the sun.

OUTDOOR SHOWERS AND BATHROOMS

PEBBLE MOSAICS AND NATURAL STONE

TIMBER DECKING

CARVED STONE BOWLS

MATERIALS AND DESIGN ELEMENTS

OPEN PAVILIONS AND OPEN PLAN LIVING

POOLS AND PONDS

BAMBOO SCREENS

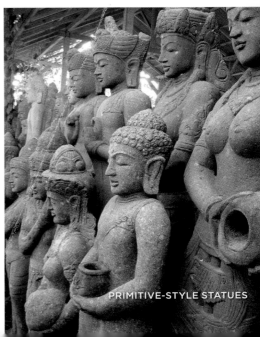
PRIMITIVE-STYLE STATUES

■ *Heliconia* cv. HELICONIA

■ *Hibiscus rosa-sinensis* HIBISCUS

■ *Bambusa* cv. BAMBC

■ *Musa* cv. ORNAMENTAL BANANA

LUSH TROPICAL PLANTS

▲ TREES & SHRUBS
■ SCREENING PLANTS
● GROUNDCOVERS

■ *Epiphyllum oxypetalum* QUEEN OF THE NIGH

● *Victoria* sp. GIANT WATER LILY

■ *Alpinia purpurata* RED GINGER

■ *Licuala grandis* LICUALA PAI

■ *Strelitzia reginae* BIRD OF PARADISE

● *Neoregelia* cv. BROMELIAD

▲■ *Dypsis lutescens* GOLDEN CANE PALM

▲ *Plumeria rubra* FRANGIPANI

■ *Alocasia brisbanensis* CUNJEVOI

● *Nymphaea* cv. WATER LILY

■ *Platycerium bifurcatum* ELKHORN FERN

● *Spathiphyllum wallisii* cv. PEACE LILY

● *Calathea zebrina* ZEBRA PLANT

HOT & DRY

JULIE NANGALA
ROBINSON

allery
gondwan

Divas of the Desert

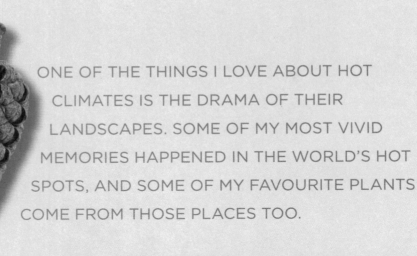

ONE OF THE THINGS I LOVE ABOUT HOT CLIMATES IS THE DRAMA OF THEIR LANDSCAPES. SOME OF MY MOST VIVID MEMORIES HAPPENED IN THE WORLD'S HOT SPOTS, AND SOME OF MY FAVOURITE PLANTS COME FROM THOSE PLACES TOO.

As a child, my family crossed the Nullarbor Plain six times on camping holidays throughout Australia. I remember looking out the window and being awestruck by the ghostly white trunks of sun-bleached mulga trees against the red earth. Such dramatic contrast. The plants looked dead but their forms were so full of life. Looking back, it probably sparked my interest in the architecture of things. It certainly opened my eyes to the beauty of a harsh, sometimes desolate, landscape.

We moved to Queensland when I was in my teens. It was a different life from Western Australia that's for sure – but every bit as outdoors. A holiday treat was going to Carnarvon Gorge between Roma and Emerald in the semi-arid southern central highlands of Queensland. This spectacular 30-kilometre long gorge is the most visited natural featue of the Carnarvon National Park. Sandstone cliffs towering up to 600 metres high flank the main gorge with Carnarvon Creek winding its way between them. Along its banks are ancient cabbage tree palms and macrozamias, mosses, ferns, flowering shrubs and eucalypts. In the smaller surrounding gorges there are remnant rainforests thriving. Today it's understandably a hub for eco-tourism.

As a young adult I moved to Las Vegas, Nevada, where I lived and worked for seven years. I'd swapped the Australian southwest for the American, the Simpson Desert for the Mojave. This new mountain-and-basin topography had earth just as red, air just as dry and heat just as relentless, and it's here I found another tree to love – the Joshua (*Yucca brevifolia*). Not many trees grow in the Mojave, but this oversized yucca is spectacularly defiant.

Joshua Tree, Nevada

Its crown of thick strappy leaves on a gnarled trunk reaches around 12 metres high, and it survives in temperatures averaging more than 35 degrees Celsius for six months out of 12, on 8 centimetres of rain a year. Nevada is part of North America's dry southwest belt that takes in Arizona and New Mexico – it's cactus country down to the Mexican border and beyond, and I've collected spiky specimens ever since my time there. Being around raw red earth for so much of my early life made me realise that gardens don't have to be green to be beautiful. The landscape taught me to look deeper to find the beauty in all landscapes.

Which is just as well. Living on the coast, as most Australians do, it's easy to forget that we occupy the driest inhabited continent on earth. However, most of the continent is semi-arid, we also have incredible climatic diversity across the land. The Northern Territory alone covers two distinct climatic zones, from the tropical top-end with its northwest monsoon rains from December to March, to the Red Centre which has one of the lowest rainfalls in the world. My last visit to Uluru (Ayers Rock) was on one of those rare occasions of wet weather. It hadn't rained on the rock for nearly 11 months and there was quite a bit of rejoicing amongst the locals. As I walked around the base, the rock's colour was changing from rust red to deeper shades, glistening and purple-tinged. The countless fissures down the sides of this quiet giant become hissing little streams – and in some areas, waterfalls, drenching and quenching the powdery ground and spinifex grass around it. The elements had carved these fissures over thousands of years, and with the rain they became these incredible sequential pools of water running down the hundreds of stone valleys – it was one of the most inspiring sights I've ever seen, and out of all the places I've been, I'm proud to have found it in Australia.

Like Australia, Mexico has great climatic diversity with forest and jungle to the south and desert to the north, and I love it for these extremes. Mexico has been the source of a lot of garden inspiration in Australia, and one of my favourite plants – the agave – comes from this part of the world. Although it resembles a succulent, it's actually a type of lily. Mexicans distil the juice of one variety – *Agave tequilana* (Weber's Blue Agave) to make tequila. In Australia, it's Agave attenuata that caught our eye a few years ago and drew attention to succulents and cacti as the beautiful,

sculptural plants they are, perfectly adapted to thrive in our climate.

I also love Mexico for the rustic beauty of its buildings that immerse you into their landscape, and the way its designers use colour so courageously. Celebrated Mexican architect Luis Barragán first drew attention to his country's adobe style of architecture in the 20th century with thick rendered walls famously painted the vibrant colours that are now synonymous with Mexican culture – pink, yellow and blue. While Barragán made striking use of colour, the houses he designed were also very private and reflective, with living areas revolving around internal walled courtyards and furnished loggias that made the transition from inside to out. This is a concept that originated in ancient Arabic architecture and a formula I incorporate wherever possible. In his own home in Mexico City, the flow from the music room, library and living room continues out to a loggia that's furnished as an indoor area. Its sheltering roof of timber beams supports the terrace off an upstairs bedroom that is completely exposed to the sun.

Loggias are part of many hot-climate cultures – in early Australia, the farmhouse verandah served the same purpose – cooling the interior, while offering a sheltered outdoor spot for relaxation. But the outdoor room has a much longer history. The Islamic gardens of the ancient Middle East were courtyards enclosed by high walls that sheltered against the desert winds and integrated with the house as the hub of family life. Literally oases in the desert, they poetically expressed a love of the outdoors and nature and were furnished with all the essential elements for life: trees for fruit and shade, flowers for colour and fragrance, elaborate water features and ornate decoration – intricate patterned screens and mosaic tiles like those we associate with Morocco, Turkey and Spain. The Islamic influence on the decorative arts of these cultures is in the repetition of geometric motifs in their designs, from pottery and carving to iron work, fabrics and frescoes.

For the last few years, PATIO has been designing the landscape for a resort that's just opened on the Spanish island of Gran Canaria. An island resort sounds like a dream job, but I got a rude shock when I first visited the site. Talk about high and dry! Gran Canaria is a mountainous volcanic island that's earned the label 'continent in miniature' for the diversity of its microclimates. The Salobre Golf Resort and Spa is situated on spectacular rocky

An internal Arabic courtyard, Dubai

ridges 5 kilometres off the coast and 275 metres above sea level. The signature plant for resorts around the world is a native of this region – the Canary Island Date Palm (*Phoenix canariensis*); however, to create a signature landscape element for the Salobre resort, we took inspiration from the rocky surrounds. We made steel cages in the shape of giant bowls, four metres in diameter, and filled them with volcanic rock from the building site, which made giant planters for another native, the candelabra cactus (*Euphorbia canariensis*). This spiky succulent grows to around 4-metres wide with stems branching out from the base, hence the name candelabra. The cacti are bedded directly into these elaborate rock vessels – the same type of rock they've always had to deal with.

Sourcing plants for the resort took me to the neighbouring island of Lanzarote, which was the most exciting cactus garden I've ever been to. We used volcanic boulders from the site in amongst the plants as sculptures and black volcanic ash as mulch. The small black stones work as a beautiful backdrop for the 10,000 or so cacti and succulents planted, including the largest golden barrel cacti (*Echinocactus grusonii*, my favourite!) I've ever seen – as big as a car bonnet. They also had the beautiful barrel cactus (*Fero cactus peninsulae* var. *townsendianus*) which is similar to the golden barrel, but red-tipped.

NATURE'S SHELTER

LOG + CABLE PLANTERS

LOG + CABLE PLANTE

A typical shade structure detailed in an innovative organic fashion becomes the centrepiece of this design. Traditional techniques and finishes have been employed to achieve a unique and modern outdoor entertaining brief.

Garden design by Jamie Durie. Illustration by Alex Augustyn.

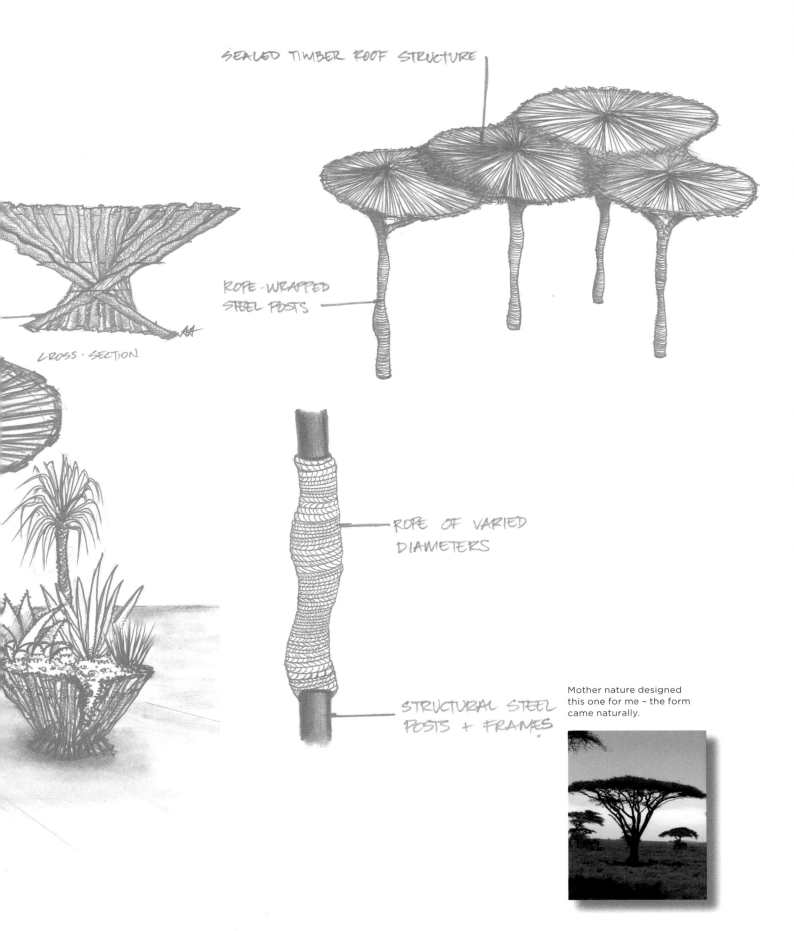

SEALED TIMBER ROOF STRUCTURE

ROPE-WRAPPED STEEL POSTS

CROSS-SECTION

ROPE OF VARIED DIAMETERS

STRUCTURAL STEEL POSTS + FRAMES

Mother nature designed this one for me – the form came naturally.

LUIS BARRAGÁN

Mexico's greatest architect and landscape designer, LUIS BARRAGÁN (1902–1988), is famous for having softened the cold lines of European Modernism with the warmth and vibrancy of Mexican colour and adobe-style aesthetics. His trademark was colouring thick, textured concrete walls pink, yellow or blue to highlight the building's geometry, and sharpen its contrast with the surroundings. He was also famous for his use of bold, dominating architecture, which has given me the confidence to incorporate oversize structures for impact in my work.

Born in Guadalajara, Mexico's 'second city' in the country's east, Barragán had been an engineer before he became an architect. This gave him the advantage of being able to resolve complex spatial and design details in a manner that appears simple – the mark of great design. He was also a very spiritual man who believed buildings should be magical and uplifting to the soul. Framing views like pictures in a landscape was another of his trademarks. He would design slim portholes in thick walls that would perfectly capture a view beyond into another, larger landscape, or he would use portholes in a series along corridors, creating a show of light and shadow that changed as the sun moved during the day.

Adapting the idea of the traditional hacienda – the massive walled estates of wealthy Mexican land-owners – Barragán's houses, though smaller in scale, offer a similar feeling of protection and privacy. He used thick, high, rendered walls to shut out the street, or to provide shelter from the elements, and focused the living areas around quiet internal courtyards.

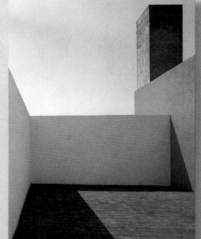

In his own studio and home in Mexico City, one room has a wall of glass looking out onto the leafy courtyard. The window is divided into four quarters, framing a part of the garden that appears quite natural, even overgrown. Here, Barragán has trained the tree just outside the window to 'lean' into the frame so that from inside the house, the garden looks like a painting. It's quite a contrast to the bolder works for which he is known. The San Cristóbal Stables in Mexico City, for example, have all his signature elements of scale, colour, light and using 'borrowed' landscape to dramatise a simple space, along with water. Central to the complex is a large reflection pool enclosed by high rendered walls coloured pink, white and red. These are sharpened against the brilliant blue sky. The only other decorations in this

Luis Barragán House and Studio

Luis Barragán House and Studio

area are trees seen through wide portholes cut into the pink wall and a cascade of water spouting into the large shallow pool from the red wall.

When I discovered Luis Barragán's work I was immediately encouraged by his use of vibrant colour. We've been quite a conservative country, but the success of his landscapes and buildings gave me added encouragement to work strong colour into concepts. Our landscape has a similar strength and quality of light that intense colour responds to so well, and vivid colour adds the kind of positive energy to a space, however great or small, that suits the Australian temperament.

Los Amantes fountain

SUNKEN TREASURE

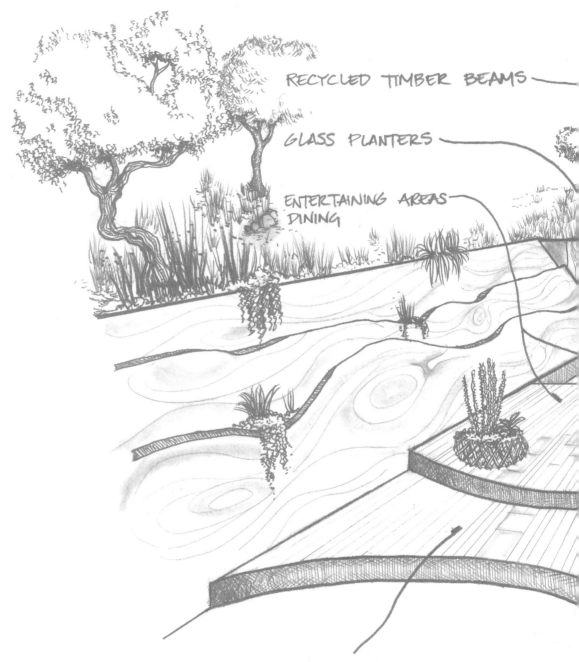

RECYCLED TIMBER BEAMS

GLASS PLANTERS

ENTERTAINING AREAS
DINING

TERRACED LEVELS

Carved into a mountain or hill, this concept creates a deep sunken garden that embraces its users within the living landscape. The recycled beams at the rear of the garden represent a deep forest view. The angled stone retaining walls create drama, and the spill-over plants add character and age to the installation.

Garden design by Jamie Durie. Illustration by Alex Augustyn.

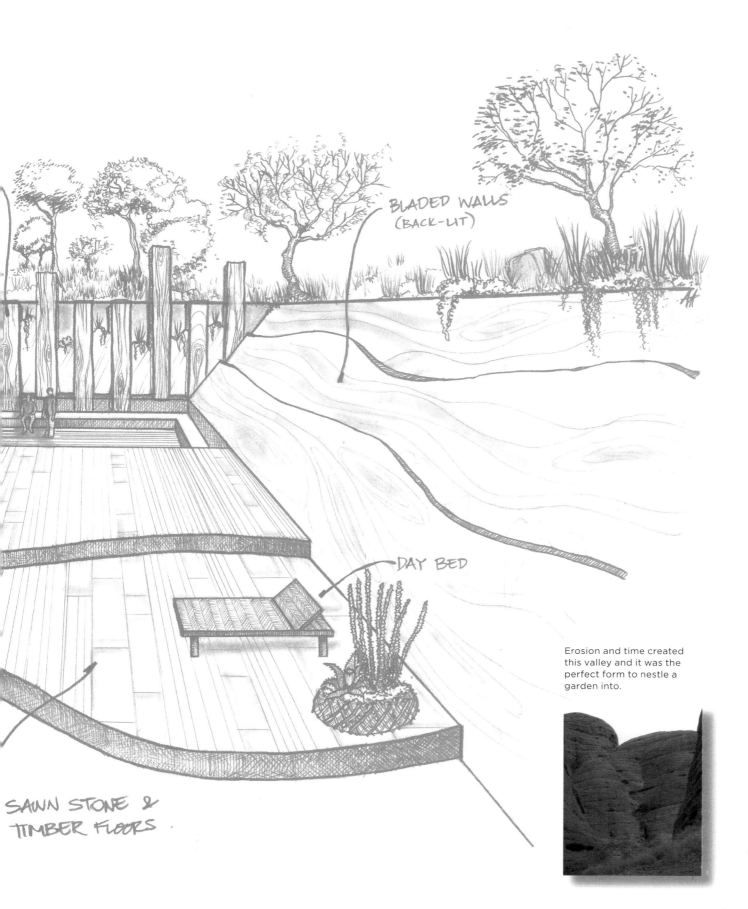

BLADED WALLS
(BACK-LIT)

DAY BED

SAWN STONE &
TIMBER FLOORS.

Erosion and time created
this valley and it was the
perfect form to nestle a
garden into.

INSIDE OUT

This outdoor living room at the rear of a renovated Sydney terrace draws influence from the modern Mexican courtyard. An extension of the indoor living room, the courtyard is enclosed by high, rendered walls painted in contrasting colours that accentuate the geometry of the space. Concertina glass doors fold to one side, allowing the inside and outside to merge under a steel overhead awning that cuts the glare from the interior.

The owners wanted a comfortable outdoor area with a spa/plunge pool and room enough to entertain or relax, with 'growing walls' to soften the space. Often when small gardens have high walls, the garden beds are in shade for most of the time, except at midday when the sun is most ferocious, so planting can be hit and miss. The solution here was to keep the plant content to a minimum, and make the space more of a furnished room decorated with garden.

A two-tiered planter box right across the rear boundary is the main built element. Tiled in large ceramic tiles in a bluestone colour, it has a narrow plunge pool in the lower tier and advanced yuccas (*Yucca*) planted in the higher. The sculptural trunks of the yuccas support multiple crowns that meet in a wild green hedge above the fence line, visually extending the garden upwards. At their base is a mulch of smooth black pebbles that complements the colour of the tiles and wall behind. Among the pebbles, bright green mosses make a pleasing contrast.

Against the adjacent white wall is a second raised planter with a wide ledge for seating. An outdoor shower is fixed to one side and a built-in barbecue on the other. A screen of black bamboo (*Phyllostachys nigra*), casts a lacy silhouette against the wall and draws the eye skyward to borrow more space.

Off centre in the courtyard is a large teak dining table on hardwood decking that is set into the concrete paving as a softening element. When not in use, the spa doubles as a fountain with water spilling from discreet blades in the bluestone tiles. Above the top tier, niches in the wall house uplights that bring the yuccas alive at night.

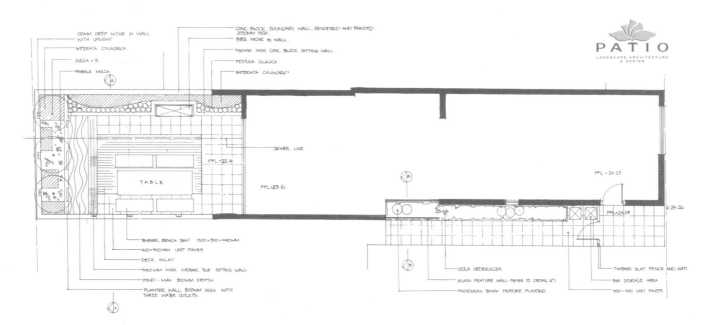

(ABOVE) The internal courtyard facing the kitchen continues the sculptural planting theme with a number of *Dracaena* planted together in a bed of black pebbles, like a reduced scaled version of the wall of yuccas at the rear.

(RIGHT) A timber duckboard tucked beside the narrow plunge pool makes a one-man perch.

(OPPOSITE) Under the shade of the giant yuccas, baby's tears are popping up between the pebbles. The ledge and walls of the plunge pool are tiled to match the bluestone colour of the rear wall.

(ABOVE) Black bamboo (*Phyllostachys nigra*) makes a lacy silhouette against the white wall. As a vertical plant, bamboo adds considerable greenery without taking up much space.

(RIGHT) Yuccas across the rear wall draw the eye upwards, bringing the sky and a neighbouring tree into the picture. The use of different colours for the courtyard walls are a nod to the Mexican influence, while the timber deck under the dining table softens the concrete and tile palette.

SHELTER ZONE

The concept behind this garden was shelter in a dry landscape such as the mountainous Mojave Desert, or the Middle East.

Journeys through rocky, barren terrain are symbolised by a maze of walls in polished marble with pillars of chunky timber, recycled from wharves, for the gateways. The grain of the stone runs at a 45-degree angle to the ground, adding to the illusion of elevation. The maze ultimately leads to an amphitheatre with high surrounding walls for shelter. In the centre of the space is a fire pit rising from a water basin, providing the ultimate mix of elements.

Planting surrounding the amphitheatre is layered with species chosen for wind- and drought-tolerance. Coastal rosemary (*Westringia fruticosa*) is hedged along the top of the amphitheatre, while *Cordyline* 'Red Star' makes a fringe in front of a curved corrugated iron wall. Raised garden beds are bordered with *Coprosma repens* 'Marble Queen', *Crassula argentea* 'Collum', *Lomandra hystrix*, *Callistemon* 'Little John', *Dianella* 'Little Rev' and 'Border Emerald'. To soften the amount of hard surfaces, green tufts of *Acorus gramineus* line up between the base of the marble slabs and the pavers. Beds are mulched with red volcanic rock.

Specimen trees here are Queensland bottle trees (*Brachychiton rupestris*) and a large dragon tree (*Draceana draco*) which help anchor the plant scheme with a windbreak. The centrepiece of the main raised planter is a huge ponytail palm (*Beaucarnea recurvata*), a Mexican relative of the yucca with a swollen base that stores the tree's food and water.

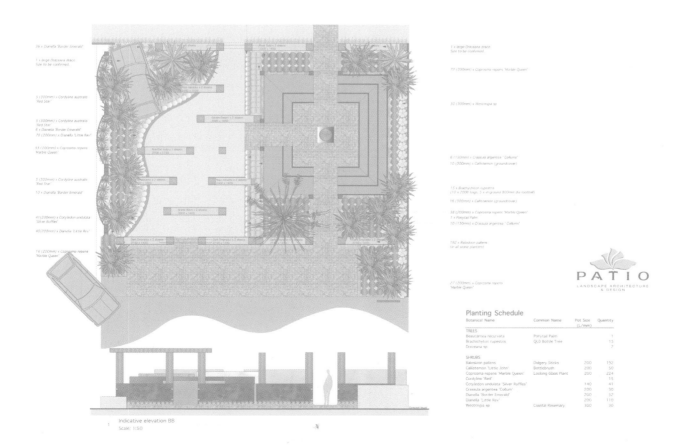

Indicative elevation BB
Scale: 1:50

HEART OF GLASS

Renovating a waterfront home in Sydney's south created two internal courtyards that needed to be user-friendly. A smaller courtyard off one of the children's bedrooms and a larger one off the kitchen offer considerably more shelter than the rear garden and pool area, so they leant themselves to being treated as outdoor rooms connected to the house, rather than gardens as such.

Based on the increasingly popular Australian vernacular style, the remodelled house is contemporary with corrugated steel cladding and extensive use of timber inside and out. The owners were keen for this to be echoed in the landscaping. This is a difficult site for gardening because of the salt-laden winds and intense heat in summer, so the planting scheme was kept simple and strong.

In the smaller courtyard a high retaining wall to one side was pre-existing but overpowering and in need of repair. Its height was softened by stepping it down with L-shaped garden beds that enabled a privacy screen to be planted. Attached to the beds

is a slatted timber bench making the area usable and inviting. Behind it, yuccas (*Yucca*) are planted in the raised bed, close enough to form a high wall as they mature. Under them is a carpet of pigface (*Carpobrotus*) – a flowering succulent used to shore up coastal dunes against erosion. The combination of vibrant greens has a cooling effect on the space, lending it shelter and intimacy.

Transforming the larger courtyard into the home's all-weather entertaining hub is an elaborate timber and glass atrium, with detailed battenwork echoing timber ceilings inside. This was built during the renovations, but a new timber deck has since replaced the tired old tiled floor, along with broad steps and a box bench at one end where a bedroom joins the space. On the boundary wall is a built-in barbecue and on the opposite side of side of the deck, along the hallway's wall of glass, is a channel of Cowra Gold pebbles for textural variation. In the gravel are bulky stone pots planted with the striking and resilient New Zealand flax (*Phormium* 'Maori Maiden').

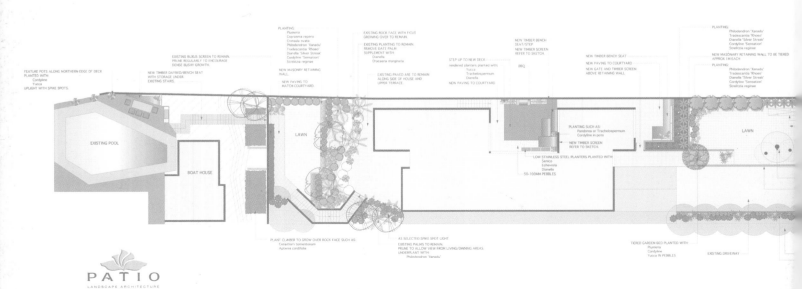

(ABOVE) Yuccas and flowering succulent pigface make a dynamic planting duo in a hot garden.

(RIGHT) To give this courtyard a more sheltered feel, the wide L-shaped garden beds have built-in benches attached, adding a sense of enclosure.

(OPPOSITE) Sculptural pieces like this Buddha statue add interest to the garden.

DESERT OASIS

The courtyard design for this garden draws on several cultural influences including the arid gardens of the ancient Middle East.

It's conceived as a water-wise urban oasis with opulence in the furnished elements and a drought-tolerant planting scheme. High white walls shelter the space and a combination of trees along the perimeter act as a windbreak and shade canopy. The Japanese maples (*Acer palmatum dissectum* 'Seiryu') are included for their striking autumn show of leaves turning yellow and red.

The focus of the design is an elaborate tiled bench that forms the retainer for the garden bed behind it. The bench curves around a copper fire pit raised on a plinth of vertical-cut lava stone. The garden bed is mulched with crushed marble rocks, ranging in size from 15mm to 200mm, and these flow down to form the base around the fire pit. The bed is planted with a mix of *Sedum* 'Chocolate Sauce', *Euphorbia* x *martinii*, *Loropetalum chinense* 'Rubrum' and society garlic (*Tulbaghia violacea*) along the curve of the tiled bench. Set into mounds of the crushed marble base around the bench, clumps of grassy *Carex buchananii* and *Helictotrichon sempervirens* spring up near a series of hand-blown glass 'rock lights'.

Using premium indoor finishes in an outdoor arena lends the space its sense of luxury and brings the inside out. The backing walls are panels of translucent white Marblo, a material used for high-end joinery and kitchen surfacing. The bench's mosaic tiles are a mix of pink and brown glass and 24-carat gold, with a high-lustre that gives this element a wet look amongst the dry landscape.

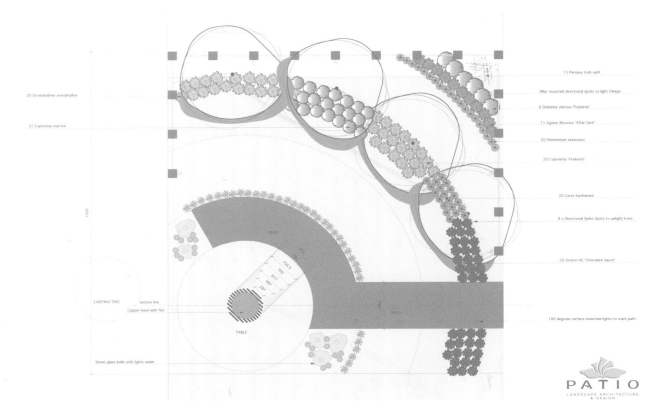

HOT & DRY
IN FOCUS

Be brave with colour, bold with form, and decorate

ornately. Building on tradition, the hot-climate garden is a

personal playground. Discover the wonderful world of succulents,

cacti and other jewels of the desert – the best friends of

the water-wise gardener. Rediscover too our own heat–

loving natives that thrive under the harshest sun.

Gardens don't need to be green

to be beautiful.

BOLD ARCHITECTURE

MOSAIC TILES

STRONG COLOURS

RECYCLED TIMBERS

MATERIALS AND DESIGN ELEMENTS

BOLD GEOMETRY

RUSTIC FINISHES

STONE

EARTH INSPIRED FINISHES

● *Agave attenuata* AGAVE

● *Banksia* 'Birthday Candles'
BIRTHDAY CANDLES BANKSIA

▲ *Yucca guatemalensis* GIANT YUC

▲ ■ *Punica granatum* POMEGRANATE

HOT & DRY PLANTS

▲ TREES & SHRUBS
■ SCREENING PLANTS
● GROUNDCOVERS

▲ ■ *Telopea speciosissima* WARAT

▲ *Beaucarnea recurvata* PONYTAIL PALM

▲ *Pachypodium lamerei* MADAGASCAR PALM

● *Aloe polyphylla* SPIRAL AL

▲ ■ *Dracaena draco* DRAGON TREE

● *Aloe arborescens* CANDELABRA ALOE

● *Carpobrotus glaucescens* COASTAL PIGFACE

▲ ■ *Leucospermum* cv. LEUCOSPERMUM

● *Echinocactus grusonii* GOLDEN BARREL CACTUS

● *Echeveria* hybrid ECHEVERIA

● *Lomandra longifolia* 'Tanika' TANIKA MAT RUSH

▲ ■ *Grevillea* hybrid GREVILLEA

▲ *Westringia fruticosa* 'Morning Light'
COASTAL ROSEMARY

Cool Temperate

IN 2004 PATIO WAS ASKED TO ENTER THE PACIFIC FLORA GARDEN COMPETITION HELD IN HAMAMATSU, IN THE SHIZUOKA PREFECTURE OF JAPAN. THE EXHIBITION RAN FROM APRIL TO OCTOBER AND I MADE THREE TRIPS DURING THE YEAR TO BUILD OUR GARDEN ENTRY AND TO EXPLORE.

The garden we entered was a stylised courtyard and deck with organically shaped timber pontoons floating, like lily pads, on water, surrounded by stepped steel crates of rocks planted with Australian natives. It won awards for both design and construction, and for inspiration.

The Japanese know what the rest of the world is just now starting to kick into, that gardening is wellbeing. They know it nurtures the soul, tending their gardens as if worshipping at the temple. I love the reverance and refinement of Japanese garden design – it has taught me the qualities of design discipline, that less is more and to embrace the natural form, and it's amazing how these qualities can be applied to almost any garden concept.

Just like Australia, Japan has a diverse topography and climate. It's one of the most geologically active areas in the world with around 60 active volcanoes throughout its main islands – its most famous, the now extinct Mt Fuji, also being its highest peak. Sharp mountain ranges rise from the coastal plains and fast-flowing rivers run quickly to the sea. Water is a force to be reckoned with. While groves of giant bamboo thrive from the tropical south to the cool-temperate north, the interior mountains are studded with birch, cedar, cypress and maple trees, and azaleas growing wild. The mountains and foothills around Kyoto, the old Imperial capital, are also studded with the country's highest concentration of Buddhist temples.

Kyoto is one of the most inspirational places I have ever been to. There are more than 2000 temples and shrines throughout the mountains, and my favourite was a tiny temple called Shisen-do, famous for its azaleas. I journeyed an hour or so to the north of the Higashiyama mountains to see Shisen-do which was built in 1641 by a scholarly samurai for his retirement. The garden is on two levels with a tea-house in

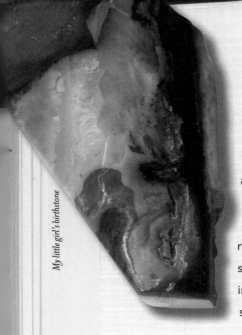

a sheltered part of the grounds. The tea house is a simple timber pavilion with beautifully detailed woodwork and shoji screens that open on three sides to unveil the garden like a landscape painting from inside. Kyoto is ringed by mountains and bisected by the Kamo River that flows north to south. Visitors flock to the temples to see spectacular cherry blossoms in spring and blazing golden maples in autumn, and to experience the serenity of the moss gardens.

The day I visited Shisen-do the garden was just brimming with life. It was raining and the azaleas, which the Japanese are so famous for, were in full flower. The rain brought out the richness and colour in the leaves and the flowers, and all the colour in the stones of the garden. I'd never really liked azaleas. They mostly seem to struggle in Australia with our humidity and our soil. But here, with their brilliant delicate flowers made luminous by the rain, they were the picture of serenity. In the West we tend to look at our dwellings as houses with doors, the Japanese look at their dwellings as roofs with no doors but gardens. The shoji screens fold back and the gardens reveal themselves with a seamless transformation between landscape and building. Sitting in the shelter of the tea house at Shisen-do, quietly taking in the rain dripping through the maples, bamboo and azaleas, was one of the most tranquil times I have ever spent in a garden. I completely lost track of time, forgot about everything else on the planet and was seduced by this ancient landscape. If I could deliver even a portion of this feeling to my clients, then my day at Shisen-do was a truly valuable lesson.

Japanese gardening is totally in tune with the plants themselves. I'm always amazed at the extraordinary pleached bamboos that reach more than 10 metres tall. Some of these groves are thousands of years old. Pleaching removes the lower branches while the higher ones are intertwined into a hedge. They do this to bamboo to show the beauty of the stem and to force the canopy to sit up high, creating an aerial screen that frames the garden and makes it intimate, enveloping you in this wall of greenery.

Similarly, the black pines are sculpted by trimming away all the lower leaves to accentuate the form of the branch and letting the top foliage grow because it receives the most light and is therefore the most ambitious part of the tree. The trunk becomes skeletal and architecturally beautiful. This practice is rooted in ancient Tibetan lore and it's purpose is to leave small 'pillows' of foliage at the end of the branches that look like clouds offset in the sky. It's a form of bonsai that takes incredible attention to detail and maintenance. There's something amazing about the idea of taking one natural form and accentuating its own individuality while at the same time stylising it to resemble (or at least symbolise) another natural form.

This approach can also be seen in their approach to landscaping. A Japanese garden represents a large landscape on a small scale. In contrast to the Western style that displays us dominating nature, the Japanese are so in awe of nature they symbolically represent it in their gardens in a balanced composition, like a landscape painting, designed to be looked at, not walked in, from within the house.

As Japanese gardens are nearly always enclosed spaces, borrowed scenery of sky, distant mountains or nearby trees is very important and may often influence the design of a garden – the first rule is that design must suit the site, not the other way around.

Rocks are the bones of the garden and the first things to be positioned. Once this is done, everything else falls into place. A lot of time and money is spent searching for the right rocks because they are believed to possess great spiritual energy. In Hamamatsu I went to a stone yard that specialises in green stone – and was staggered to see thousands of pieces to choose from. The stone's shape, size and markings are all important characteristics – the more weathered and aged and unique, the better.

Water has many symbolic meanings in the Japanese garden but wherever it is used, it must have a visible source, a journey and a destination – just as a river flows to the sea. You can have a waterfall, but not a fountain, for instance, because it would never occur naturally. Water symbolises spiritual cleansing and often a garden will have a small stone water basin to represent the *tsukubai*, a basin of water placed near a temple gate so visitors can cleanse their mouths and hands before proceeding.

Plants are limited in the Japanese garden and each one is placed for a reason. It's a completely unselfish schedule they work on with endless patience for things to grow – not like us at all. And there is also no compulsion to fill every corner. The empty space, *ma*, is important to help define the elements in the garden. Unlike the western model of gardens as physical playgrounds, the Japanese garden is more a sanctuary or separate world for the mind and soul to wander freely.

Though these gardens are enclosed they are not always exclusive. Fences and screens allow for 'hide and reveal' – a specialty of Japanese design. A small window may be cut into a fence to tease a passer-by with a tiny glimpse of the space within. Inversely the window may be for the benefit of those within the garden, offering a view of a space beyond. Nobody frames a garden view quite like the Japanese, and I'm borrowing the idea for the front room of my new house. It's a tatami room with a window in the screen wall revealing a small bonsai garden on the steps outside. The window will be very low to the ground, and the angle will bring the sky into the backdrop.

One very important landscape designer, and one of my favourites, is Kyoto-based Atsushi Akenuki. He worked with the Chinese-born modernist architect I.M. Pei on the Miho Museum in Shiga prefecture and now manages Japan's best-known *ryokan* (traditional guesthouse), the Tawaraya. He is also responsible for creating some of the country's most exciting contemporary gardens, most of them in tiny spaces, which are designed to be experienced as a series of composed views. These often end with an exquisitely framed garden view that from the inside makes you feel like you are one with the garden itself.

While designers in Japan are working with fresh directions in landscape design – experimenting with plants, materials and form, there is still an unmistakable Zen quality to contemporary garden design. For many centuries in Japan, Buddhist monks were the makers and keepers of gardens and it's no coincidence that today, one of Japan's most inspiring landscape architects, Shunmyo Masuno, is also a Zen priest. There are many books about Masuno's work, and he also wrote the introduction to one of my favourite books, *The Modern Japanese Garden*, where he talks about the Zen garden in a most inspiring way: 'The path to simplicity in a Zen garden whether ancient or modern is to express nature in a pure form'. To achieve this very essence, says Masuno, we must not continue adding to a space, but instead 'use simple materials to express everything'.

Traditional welcome stones

CLEAR SPACE

WATER-FIRE FEATURE

STONE BENCH

To draw people into the area a large magnet in the form of a combined water feature-fireplace was placed in the centre of the clearing. This provides a focal point in the garden, adding interest as well as warmth to a typically cool-climate forest retreat. Heavy insulation prevents the water from heating up, while the aspects of water and fire, placed at a 90°-angle to each other, allow the users a choice of view depending upon where they sit within the garden.

Garden design by Jamie Durie.
Illustration by Alex Augustyn.

This simplistic concept is inspired by natures-own creation – the forest glade.

INNER SANCTUM

The owners of this Melbourne garden had seen an exhibition garden at the Melbourne International Flower and Garden Show designed by PATIO and were inspired by it. The design was conceived as a sanctuary, built into a long narrow urban space, such as you might find on the side of a house. At the end of a reflection pond, a simple yoga pavilion was reached by narrow stepping stones threaded through a maze of mass planting. It was a garden for just one person seeking privacy and peace in a confined space.

The owners of this garden wanted a similar feeling of sanctuary for their space, with a day bed instead of a yoga pavilion, to be enjoyed by two people not one. They wanted a flexible area for outdoor entertaining and screening to hide the garage and driveway, and a visual link from a small internal courtyard to the rear garden using water features.

Inspiration for this design comes from the Japanese philosophy of stylising nature into miniature landscapes as a focus for meditation, and water features are key to this. The internal courtyard has, as its backdrop, backlit frosted glass windows that lead to a bathroom. This called for a sculptural element at the end of the pond – a wrought iron bench – to cast a silhouette at night. The larger pond ends with a timber built-in day bed, backed by a wall of horizontal decking that hides the garage.

Planting beds are divided into rectangles, like a sushi tray. Each is massed with contrasting forms and textures for colour and flowers all year round. The crab apple tree, *Malus hyphensis* 'Hupeh Crab', is the star performer, offering yellow fruit, pink blossoms or silver branches, depending on the time of year. The burgundy-tipped leaves of *Loropetalum chinense* 'China Pink' cascade along the edge of the larger pond with mauve-flowering convolvulus (*Convolvulus sabatius* ssp. *mauritanicus*) opposite. The screening hedge of sacred bamboo (*Nandina domestica*) brings red berries and white flowers, while in the cool internal courtyard, white arum lilies (*Zantedeschia aethiopica*) are nearly always in flower.

For harmony, paving is the same charcoal colour throughout the design but made up of different formats and stones: large black limestone squares, rectangles of lava stone which turns mossy in the shadows, black granite and bluestone. A single charcoal-coloured concrete paver moulded as a stylised flower sits in among the groundcovers as a quiet symbol. Beside the rear door is another symbol – a small granite water basin to represent the Japanese tsukubai.

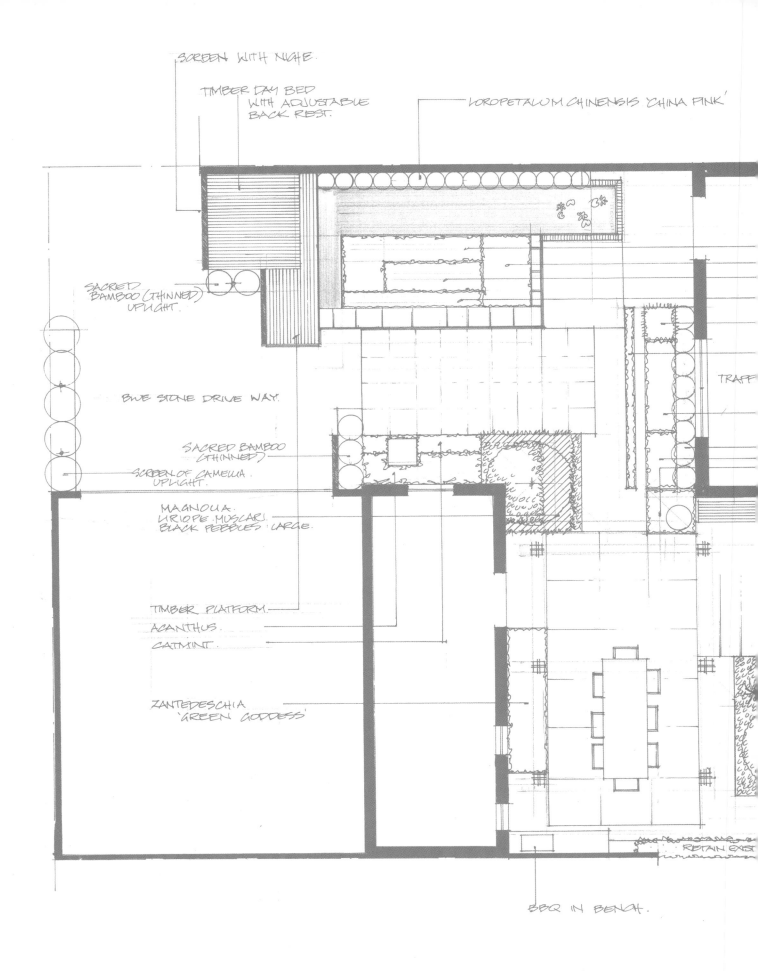

SCREEN WITH NICHE.

TIMBER DAY BED
WITH ADJUSTABLE
BACK REST.

LOROPETALUM CHINENSIS 'CHINA PINK'

SACRED
BAMBOO (THINNED)
UPLIGHT.

BLUE STONE DRIVE WAY.

SACRED BAMBOO
(THINNED)

SCREEN OF CAMELLIA.
UPLIGHT.

TRAFF

MAGNOLIA.
LIRIOPE MUSCARI.
BLACK PEBBLES : LARGE.

TIMBER PLATFORM.

ACANTHUS.

CATMINT.

ZANTEDESCHIA
'GREEN GODDESS'

RETAIN EXIS

BBQ IN BENCH.

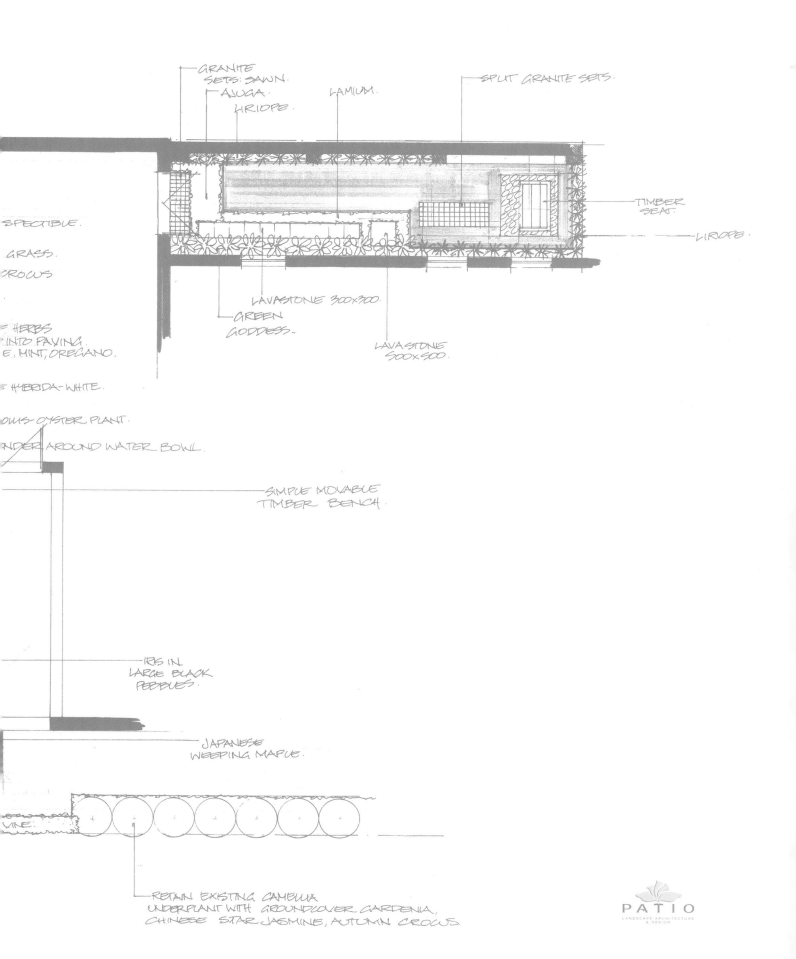

GRANITE
SETS: SAWN.
AJUGA.
LIRIOPE.

LAMIUM.

SPLIT GRANITE SETS.

TIMBER
SEAT.

LIRIOPE.

SPECTIBLE.

GRASS.

CROCUS

HERBS
INTO PAVING.
E, MINT, OREGANO.

HYBRIDA-WHITE.

OWS-OYSTER PLANT.

NDER AROUND WATER BOWL.

LAVASTONE 300x300.

GREEN
GODDESS.

LAVASTONE
500x500.

SIMPLE MOVABLE
TIMBER BENCH.

IRIS IN
LARGE BLACK
PEBBLES.

JAPANESE
WEEPING MAPLE.

VINE.

RETAIN EXISTING CAMELLIA
UNDERPLANT WITH GROUNDCOVER GARDENIA,
CHINESE STAR JASMINE, AUTUMN CROCUS.

PATIO
LANDSCAPE ARCHITECTURE
& DESIGN

(LEFT) A granite water basin symbolises a Japanese ritual. In Japanese tradition, water is the source of ritual cleansing, said to give health and wisdom and remove the spiritual grime of everyday life.

(RIGHT) A broader view showing mass planting in the garden beds which are divided up like a sushi box, as well the larger of the two reflection ponds.

(OPPOSITE) The smaller pond fills the sheltered internal courtyard, fringed by arum lilies and lily turf (*Liriope*). At the far end are opaque windows to the bathroom and a water-wall of stacked stone that's uplit at night from within the pond.

(ABOVE) The timber day bed is sheltered on three sides with horizontal slatted walls and a recessed niche for ornaments or for simply resting drinks out of the way.

(RIGHT) Seen from across the garden, the day bed is also screened from view by thick plantings of contrasting coloured foliage and flowers such as the burgundy-leaved *Loropetalum chinense* 'China Pink' along the sunny wall and mauve-flowering convolvulus opposite.

ZEN INFLUENCE

This Melbourne garden crosses cultural and climatic boundaries with a Japanese-inspired zen design and predominantly native plant scheme. Sited at the rear of an old terrace house with a contemporary extension, the garden bears the brunt of midday summer sun and extended periods of shade.

Designed as a contemplative courtyard to be viewed from the kitchen, living area and bedrooms, it is also intended as a space where the owners, a professional couple, can entertain clients if they wish. The garden needed to be sympathetic to both old and new sections of the house. The owners wanted a water feature that was relaxing without being noisy, and they needed vehicle access for a small car, which meant paving would be pivotal to the design.

Black limestone paving is laid in an ashlar pattern (using stones of equal thickness but unequal length) which gives the illusion of movement but not in any particular direction. To tie in with the foundations of the house, remnant bluestone from the site makes a sculptural platform for the timber day bed which sits like an altar with a reflection pool at its base. Limestone steppers, also in an ashlar pattern, are set into the pond, while around the courtyard selected stones are replaced with pockets of groundcover plants so the garden appears to pop up between the pavers.

In perimeter beds mulched with quartz gravel are *Banksia*, tussock rush (*Juncus usitatus*), knobby club rush (*Isolepis nodosa*), kangaroo paw (*Anigozanthus*), *Leucadendron* and cardboard palm (*Zamia furfuracea*). Groundcovers include natives *Chorizema*, *Viola hederacea* and *Scleranthus biflorus* – a tight green mounding carpet with tiny white flowers in summer. Either side of the day bed are young *Robinia* trees whose lime green leaves are a striking contrast against the red ochre of the rendered courtyard walls – a colour chosen to lend warmth to the interior and match a painting inside the house. The geometry of the paving is echoed in patterns on the timber vehicle entry and in beams interspersed along the red wall displaying pots of flowering cut leaf daisy (*Brachscome multifida*).

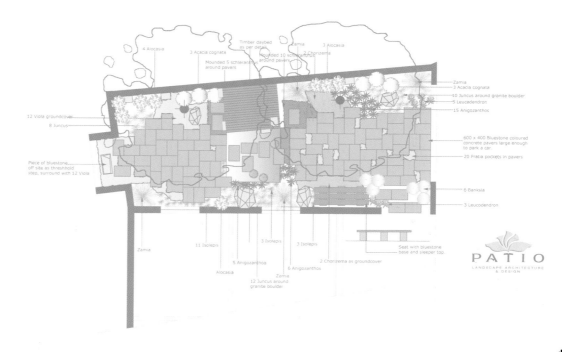

(OPPOSITE) Stepping stones in the pond allow the ashlar pattern of the paving to appear continuous with the water visually receding while the garden seems to spring up from the paving in tiny pockets of groundcovers.

(ABOVE) Around a granite boulder in the gravel are tussock rush (*Juncus usitatus*) and elephants' ears.

(RIGHT) A vibrant ochre red was mixed for the courtyard walls, to match a favourite painting of the owners'. The timber gate for car access is detailed with a similar asymmetric pattern to the black limestone paving.

NATURAL GEOMETRY

This compact garden behind a large Sydney house packs a lot into a small space. Its design is based on the intersecting geometries of soft and hard landscape forms to give the illusion of space, with a sense of order and calm.

The Federation house had been extended but the garden never resolved. Pre-existing was a large jacaranda in the northwest corner, and the owners had planted a screening hedge of *Viburnum* across the rear boundary and a row of evergreen ash trees (*Fraxinus uhdei*) along the high side of the fence before they called for help.

They wanted a more usable outdoor area off the music room plus as large a swimming pool as could be squeezed onto the wedge-shaped site. It needed to be long enough for lap swimming, with a shallow area for kids and a wide, long bench seat under the water. They wanted a sundeck by the pool and a variety of interesting foliage in the plant scheme, but nothing too tricky to maintain: 'The neatness of a formal garden, without the formality and fuss'.

A raised timber pontoon nestles into a corner beside the pool under the ash trees, with accessible storage that conceals the filter and cleaning equipment. The ash trees are underplanted with herbs and creeping fig (*Ficus pumila*) that will eventually cover the side fence. The viburnum is fringed with dwarf gardenias (*Gardenia radicans*) for scent. At the other end of the pool is a raised timber planter with shore juniper (*Juniperus conferta*), and a small, cool lawn flanked by walls of *Camellia sasanqua* hedged around the jacaranda.

The courtyard off the music room is paved with a pumice-coloured New Zealand volcanic stone that continues around the pool. Along the safety fence, a row of *Magnolia* 'Little Gem' trees is underplanted for foliage contrast with silver-leafed, yellow-flowering treasure flowers (*Gazania*).

While the family gets a lot more use out of the garden, visually, its pleasing geometry is designed to be enjoyed from above. Upstairs off the living room is a sundeck where large copper pots of *Cordyline* 'Red Star' make a privacy screen for a pair of sunlounges – the owners' favourite spot for taking in the view.

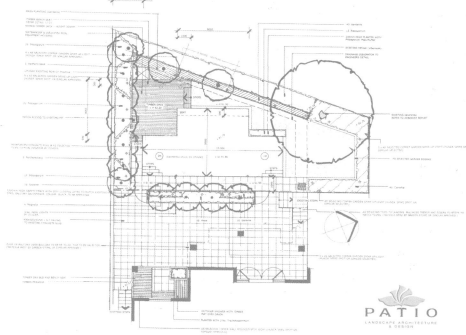

(OPPOSITE) The pool works around the angle of the wedge-shaped yard. To accentuate its geometry, the palette of materials is kept minimal – timber and pale stone for hard surfaces, with plant material restricted to shades of green.

(BELOW) The sculptural limbs of the evergreen ash trees beside the pontoon. The ground plane is planted with hebes (*Hebe*). The timber wall hides the pool filter and cleaning equipment.

(ABOVE) A raised timber pontoon for sunbathing goes right to the pool edge. Level changes add volume to small spaces.

(RIGHT) The pontoon steps down to volcanic stone coping. Inside the pool is a long, wide bench used as a step out for smaller children, or as a seat.

COOL TEMPERATE
IN FOCUS

Simplicity and tranquility. A quiet, reflective space to read or meditate. A large landscape in a small space – a place where time slows down. Artful geometry influences order and calm. Essential elements: rock, water, plants, scenery, ornaments. Water used as reflection pools with a still or just-broken surface. Place rocks with good intent. Use trees to balance light and shade, plants for foliage colour and flower. Use refined materials, restrain design.

GRANITE WATER VESSELS

STEPPING STONES

TIMBER SCREENING

ASYMMETRIC PAVING PATTERNS

MATERIALS AND DESIGN ELEMENTS

PEBBLES

TIMBER DECKS

REFLECTION PONDS

DECORATIVE BOULDERS

▲ *Robinia pseudoacacia* 'Frisia'
GOLDEN ROBINIA

▲ ■ *Camellia sasanqua* SASANQUA CAMELLIA

■ *Vitis vinifera* 'Alicante Bouch
ORNAMENTAL GRA

Prunus serrulata 'Ichiyo
JAPANESE FLOWERING CHERRY

COOL TEMPERATE
PLANTS

▲ TREES & SHRUBS
■ SCREENING PLANTS
● GROUND COVERS

● *Loropetalum chinense* 'China Pi
CHINA PINK FRINGE FLOW

▲ *Acer palmatum* JAPANESE MAPLE

● *Heuchera* cv. CORAL BELLS

● *Cycas revoluta* JAPANESE SAGO PA

▲ ■ *Magnolia grandiflora* 'Little Gem'
LITTLE GEM MAGNOLIA

● *Juniperus conferta* SHORE JUNIPER

▲ *Malus* cv. CRABAPPLE

● *Liriope muscari* LILY TURF

● MOSS

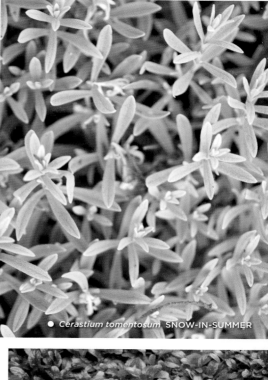
● *Cerastium tomentosum* SNOW-IN-SUMMER

■ *Nandina domestica* SACRED BAMBOO

● *Sedum spectabile* ICE PLANT

● *Ajuga reptans* CARPET BUGLE WEED

Sensory

The week's h

Small C
Ten If you
mothers r
beautifully

Six Feet Under
darkest episode
It's Nate's birthd
short supply as th
its demons.

Nerds FC, Friday, 7.3
geeks ba

Sarala in the film W

FILM

Water Deepa Mehta's
cloaks its polemics in
abundance of seducti
about Indian life. None
her outrage at the pov
humiliation forced upor
widows is unmistakabl
Ray stars, but much of
story is seen throu
of Chuyia
year-old
without kr
husband. S

'Imagination is more important than knowledge.' ALBERT EINSTEIN

CIRQUE DU SOLEIL

CIRQUE DU SOLEIL AT BELLAGIO

ALEGRIA
CIRQUE DU SOLEIL

VIP

BMW

AS DESIGNERS WE TRY TO ENGINEER GARDENS FOR PEOPLE TO ENJOY, BUT I THINK MOST OF US RESPOND MORE TO MAGIC THAN DESIGN. I CERTAINLY DO. I LOVE SEEING SOMETHING LEFT OF CENTRE OR UNEXPECTED, AND FOR INSPIRATION I ALWAYS LOOK TO THE WORK OF ARTISTS.

One of my favourite gardens in the world is the Central Garden at the Getty Center in Los Angeles. It's such a playful garden, in many ways it's more like an abstract landscape than a real one. This is because it was designed by the American artist Robert Irwin who approached the project more like he was painting a picture than building a garden.

For me it's a horticulturally defiant garden with plants used in unexpected ways that create sheer delight. In Robert Irwin's garden there's a maze of pink azaleas planted in the middle of a pond that took my breath away. Azaleas are a sensitive cool-climate plant, but here, in the Southern Californian desert, they've been hedged into a maze that's sunk into water – surrounded by their own reflection. As a landscaper I'd never think of using them that way – and that's what's so exciting. If I was doing a water garden I'd think first of using waterlilies, papyrus, bull grass – plants that I know would work well. Irwin didn't think that way. He wanted to make evocative shapes and challenging relationships between the natural and artificial elements. There's nothing more important than having your senses challenged to fire the imagination.

A garden that I hope is playful in a different way is the Sensory Garden at The Children's Hospital at Westmead in Sydney. It's well-documented that gardens are good not just for the soul, but for our health as well, so as a parent and ambassador for Plan International I was very keen to do a garden to help with children recovering from illness. Kids are often our greatest teachers and designing this garden allowed me to reconnect with my own inner child.

We designed it as a multisensory play space to motivate and encourage healing and rehabilitation with a series of private nooks for outdoor therapy sessions and family visits. A sensory environment uses sounds, smells, tactile impressions and visual surprises. When our senses are switched on, we use them more and this is a vital part of therapy.

Children love to be fascinated and they love exploring – it opens up their imaginations. The garden has lots of little enchanted areas to attract and distract the kids – literally leading them up the garden path! Kids also like to stake out their own patch of turf so each little spot in the garden has a different feel. Some areas have a masculine feel with the planting more bold and robust. Some have a fragile feel, like fairy dells with carpets of delicate moss and native violets, ferns and lacy foliage plants.

Linking the areas is a meandering pathway so there's always something new to discover just around the bend. No two kids will experience this garden in the same way and that's part of its magic. Like the children it's designed for, the garden is still quite young, but we've laid down some good foundations, and all it needs is time and love.

The nurturing feel of a garden can also come from the materials used in it. Recycled timbers lend an earthy, tactile presence with a sense of history and age. The patina of age is especially valuable in small spaces where we experience the materials at close range – too many shiny new surfaces can feel cold and uninviting and harsh against the plants.

The British installation artist Andy Goldsworthy has a unique way of using materials from nature – sticks and stones, sand or clay, ice and even snow – which make you look at these elements with fresh eyes so they seem like objects of great beauty, which of course they are. He creates sculptures in outdoor natural settings from raw materials that he picks in response to each site. The sculptures are not designed to dominate the surrounding nature, they are there to underline its beauty and draw attention to the energy and detail of the material. What's also fascinating about them is their transience. The sculptures only last long enough to be photographed before he dismantles them, or leaves the more fragile ones to simply weather away. This gentle reminder of nature's impermanence is a challenge to designers because we go to great lengths to ensure that we build things to last.

Sculpting form with natural material is such a gratifying creative outlet – Sasha Reid mentors me...

While it may not be practical or even appropriate to build everything from old materials, feature elements such as screens made from old timber battens where the wood is slightly beaten up and bleached of colour bring great character to a space. Alternatively, timber palings with layers of paint still on them are interesting additions to the material mix. Metals too can lend warming effects – copper aged with green swirls of oxidisation, or rusted ironwork, panels, old gates, even window grilles, bring rich colour and texture that grow richer with age.

I recently visited the studio of Sydney sculptor Sasha Reid, whose chunky recycled timber and steel objects are typified by *Big Mouth*, a work that first appeared in Sydney's Sculpture by the Sea exhibition and made a colourful splash a couple of years ago. He has a number of large-scale public commissions, including a memorial to the victims of the Bali bombing, *Reclaiming Spirit* at Dolphin Point in Coogee, New South Wales, and several works in Chicago. His smaller works, tactile kinetic sculptures carved and forged from salvaged timber, stone and steel, are just as engaging because they invite us to reach out and touch them. They are gutsy and raw, but with a refined edge and a sense of the familiar. One series of sculptures resembles prehistoric tools – spears and axes, mallets and hammers, finely poised on a fulcrum; the kind you'd see in a museum. But Reid doesn't like the 'look but don't touch' mentality of a lot of art. He wants us to feel them because making them is a very hands-on process and he wants us to share that experience, to feel the energy of the material and the maker's mark.

SHIFTING WATER

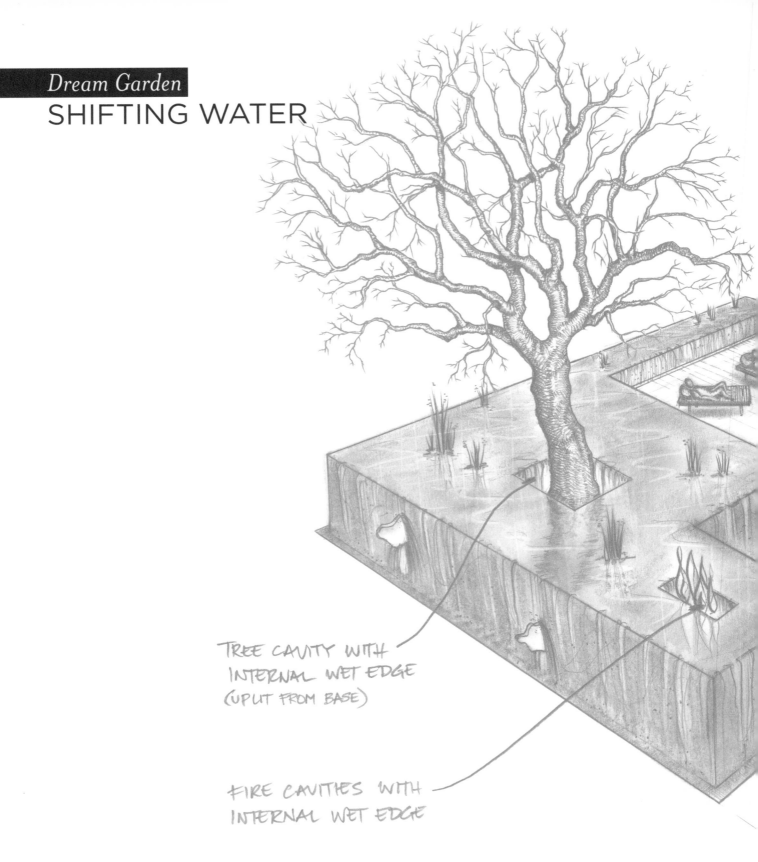

TREE CAVITY WITH
INTERNAL WET EDGE
(UPLIT FROM BASE)

FIRE CAVITIES WITH
INTERNAL WET EDGE

Water is commonly used as a feature in a garden; however, this idea
reverses the approach, accentuating the fire and trees by providing
structurally intimate surrounds, completely coated in shifting water.

Garden design by Jamie Durie. Illustration by Alex Augustyn.

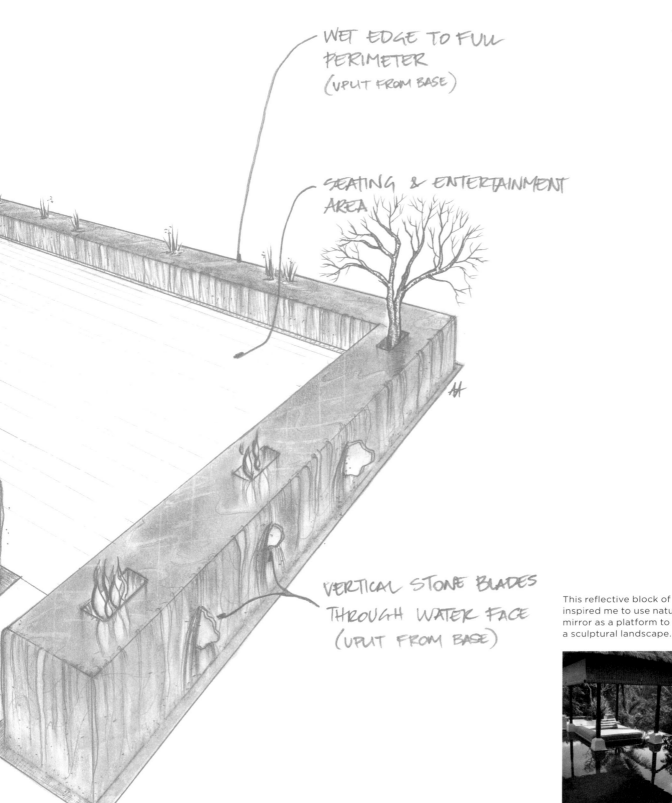

WET EDGE TO FULL
PERIMETER
(UPLIT FROM BASE)

SEATING & ENTERTAINMENT
AREA

VERTICAL STONE BLADES
THROUGH WATER FACE
(UPLIT FROM BASE)

This reflective block of water inspired me to use nature's mirror as a platform to grow a sculptural landscape.

ROBERT IRWIN

Azaleas, Getty Garden

Artist ROBERT IRWIN describes the garden he created for the Getty Center in Los Angeles as 'a sculpture in the form of a garden aspiring to be art'. The Getty Garden emphasises a natural ravine between the Getty Museum and the Research Institute with a stream that snakes its way down to the plaza and central pool with views out over the city. It's a huge site, like a university campus, and the museum is a stark, white travertine building that sprawls across the ridge. It was designed by Modernist architect Richard Meier, and it's such a controlled building, devoid of decoration, I think they had the right idea getting an artist to landscape around it. Irwin gave the landscape a sense of adventure and discovery with some great visual illusions, playing with colour and texture, but also with scale.

Irwin was a part of a Californian art movement in the 1960s called 'Light and Space'. Artists in this movement experimented with technology to build installations that manipulated scale to alter our perceptions of space and give those who saw their work a provocative sensory experience.

The Getty Garden gives many impressions. Viewed from above, it looks like a painting full of intricate colours and textures interwoven – flowering trees, exotic grasses, reflection ponds. On deep terraced steps there are massive concrete bowls filled with flowers and succulents. So much about this place is about using over-scaled forms, it's a bit of a 'Land of the Giants' experience – especially for me!

Irwin 'painted' natural forms with built ones. The stream that unifies the scene is lined with slate and crossed at several points by paths for the disabled. Even without water, the riverbed has a sense of movement because of the huge slate blocks that stand on edge along its course – they look like schools of fish travelling downstream and the texture

Ingenius steel climbing trees, Getty Garden

and detail is awesome. On the upper edge of the central pool, a stand of metal tree-like frames support bright pink bougainvillea in a spectacular flowering canopy. With time and taming this vigorous tropical climber over the structures will, from above, look like flamboyant flowering trees.

The cacti garden especially intrigued me. Irwin took his cue from the topography of the site. One wing of the building goes right to the edge of the ridge, overlooking Los Angeles. He used huge blade walls to divide the planting and draw your eye out over that ridge to the city view below. Between the blades are groves of towering Euphorbia, and magnificent, yellow-spiked golden barrel cactus (*Echinocactus grusonii*). These are some of my favourite plants and I was more than a little influenced by this spectacle when I designed the cacti garden for Sydney's Royal Botanic Gardens.

While some of the elements at the garden mimic nature with artificial forms, some of them defy it. It's certainly an unconventional garden and the horticulturalists working with Irwin would have been anxious over the logistics of his vision. I can only imagine the arguments they must have had – I guess great things don't come easily. Apart from the uplifting experience of being in a place where so much seems improbable, the sheer audacity of the Getty Garden makes anything seem possible. If there is only one design lesson I can take from Robert Irwin, it is to always push the creative bounds of your designs: try the impossible, blend the old in a new way, and always seek out new techniques to realise them.

A flying cactus and succulent garden, Getty Garden

ANDY GOLDSWORTHY

English environmental artist ANDY GOLDSWORTHY has been travelling through Britain, Japan, the United States and Australia since the late 1970s, creating organic sculptures in nature, using natural materials. His raw materials are mostly leaves, branches, sand and stone, even ice and snow – nature's detritus – and he sculpts them into free-form shapes decided upon in direct response to the landscape.

Sometimes the earth itself is Goldsworthy's raw material and he carves circles, lines and spirals into its surface – shapes from nature representing the molecules that bind organisms together or fault-lines that tear the earth apart.

Some of his sculptures are all about colour, which he sees as a form of energy. In Dumfriesshire, UK, he threaded the purple flowers of foxgloves into long stalks and made a snaking thread of them through a field of lush, green bracken fern. In New York's Storm King Sculpture Park, he laid out a bright yellow 'dandelion line' across a cool, green lawn. I love the courage an artist brings to a project.

One of the things I find inspiring about Goldsworthy's work is he's such a purist with materials. He'll take a single medium, stone for instance, and work with it over a long period of time, exploring every aspect of how to shape it, stack it, pull it apart and put it back together, and I take that approach in my work.

The other interesting thing about his work is that, unlike a lot of sculpture, which by nature is permanent, Goldsworthy's are fleeting. His early works were usually constructed in a single day (he had help for the larger ones) then photographed and either dismantled or, for the more fragile ones, left to weather away. The photographs in his published books are the only remaining record of their existence – and of course the artist's memory. The humbling message is that while humans can control nature for a short time, eventually, nature controls us; like his sculptures set in the wild, we are part of a much bigger picture.

Andy Goldsworthy photographs his ice pyramids in the Arctic Circle

AERIAL GARDEN

LANTERNS

The roof is often forgotten in an outdoor space. This concept floats the garden in unique vessels suspended from the roof; accentuating their spatial presence and the indentations in the deck below. The indentations both mirror the circular form of the plant vessels and create intimate sunken lounges, illuminated from above to bring ambience to the space.

Garden design by Jamie Durie. Illustration by Alex Augustyn.

GIANT
CONCRETE
PLANTERS

DECK
INDENTS

Pot plants are such a
common part of today's
landscapes – but how often
do they fly?

HARBOUR DECK

This penthouse rooftop garden takes in a commanding view of Sydney's Elizabeth Bay. It tucks right into the point of a rooftop that's shaped like the bow of a ship. The building is one of Sydney's new-generation apartments where all eyes are focused on the view, so it was important for the landscaping to focus attention on the harbour, rather than distract from it.

The rooftop space had been inhospitable and did nothing to encourage the owners outside. At around 220 square metres, it was large and bland and quite exposed to the heat and wind, and thanks to light-coloured ceramic tiles on the floor, it was also much too glary for comfort. To transform the space, a timber easy-deck was laid straight over the top of the tiles, set back around 2 metres off the balustrade for safety. Rows of planter boxes divide the terrace into a series of smaller outdoor rooms for dining, sunbaking and entertaining, and these are filled with sun-tough lavender (*Lavandula*), mat rushes (*Lomandra* 'tanika'), shore juniper (*Juniperus conferta*) and variegated star jasmine (*Trachelospermum jasminoides* 'Tricolor') left to hang as a fringe, not trained up a trellis. All are low-growing, except a screen

of New Zealand Christmas bush (*Metrosideros excelsa*), planted to one side for privacy and as a windbreak.

Because it's an apartment building, none of the landscape is structurally attached to the roof. All the elements are completely removable for maintenance and repairs to the building. Planters are lightweight marine-grade stainless steel, made in sections small enough to transport in an elevator. Even the easy-deck is removable. The individual timber 'tiles' clip together on top of the existing tiled floor with plastic saddles that raise the deck just enough to accommodate the drip-irrigation pipes and allow stormwater to drain away.

In the same way artist Robert Irwin used angles at the Getty Garden (pages 138–139) to draw the eye to the view of Los Angeles below, this deck and most of the planter boxes run in a straight line, pointing out to the bay. The exception is the row of *Lomandra* that curves in line with the balustrade to visually soften its feet. Among the creature comforts on the terrace is a wavy built-in day bed, sandwiched between two planters for sunbaking in privacy. Even this is kept low so the eye rolls right over it to the view.

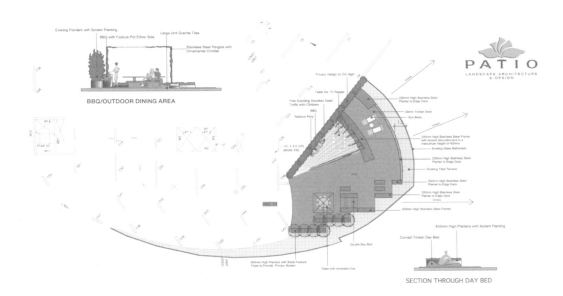

BBQ/OUTDOOR DINING AREA

SECTION THROUGH DAY BED

(ABOVE) Planter boxes made from marine-grade stainless steel are filled with the drought-tolerant rush (*Lomandra* 'Tanika') and a mulch of river pebbles.

(LEFT) Furnishings and plants on the deck are kept low so as not to impede the water view. While the angles of the deck draw the eye to the balustrade and beyond, twin totem sculptures carved from Hebel block nestle among the shore juniper as a visual anchor for the deck itself.

NATURAL REMEDY

The garden at the The Children's Hospital at Westmead in western Sydney, New South Wales, is a therapeutic space for young patients and their families to visit and play and take their minds off their challenging days inside the hospital. Many of the children in the Westmead oncology unit are long-term patients, spending months at a time in hospital, so their opportunities for outdoor play or contact with nature are limited.

Although still in its infancy, the garden is conceived as a multisensory garden using sights, colour, sounds, smells and tactile impressions to stimulate the senses. There are many aims for this garden – among them, to have a pleasant environment that helps motivate the kids to participate in therapy, physiotherapy, and relaxation techniques such as yoga, music therapy and Tai Chi. It's also simply meant to be a fun space to play where healing is encouraged by stimulating the senses.

Composed of a series of nooks to accommodate individual therapy sessions and family visits, the garden is set out along an 'experience trail' – a long meandering path that winds through the garden linking one area to the next. Along the path there are seating areas, grassed areas and decked areas, corralled by low walls painted in vibrant colours. The built structures are softened with cushions covered in bright printed fabric and areas planted for scent, colour and textured foliage, with staff at the hospital adding to the garden with cheerful animal sculptures that arrive regularly. The animals find their way in amongst the plants, waiting to be discovered.

At the end of the meandering path is a water tower with a difference. It's a blue-tiled column with windchimes hanging around it from above. Water runs down the column into a narrow catchment at the base but there's no landscaping around it, just plenty of room for wheelchairs or hospital beds to move right up to the column so the kids can put their hands into the running stream of water – or reach up to clang the windchime which always brings a big beaming smile. The multisensory garden, nicknamed Percy's Place, was made possible with the help of a bequeath from Mr Percy Minard, whose family officially opened the garden in May 2006, and a host of other contributors whose names are also on display in the garden.

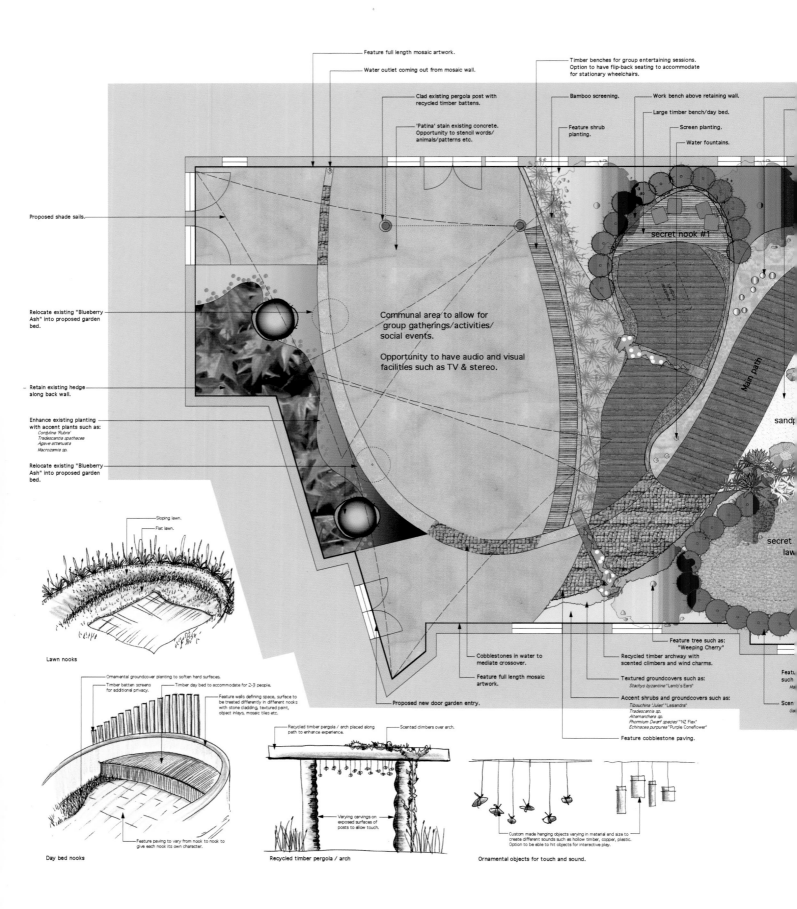

Feature full length mosaic artwork.

Water outlet coming out from mosaic wall.

Timber benches for group entertaining sessions.
Option to have flip-back seating to accommodate for stationary wheelchairs.

Clad existing pergola post with recycled timber battens.

Bamboo screening.

Work bench above retaining wall.

'Patina' stain existing concrete.
Opportunity to stencil words/animals/patterns etc.

Feature shrub planting.

Large timber bench/day bed.

Screen planting.

Water fountains.

Proposed shade sails.

secret nook #1

Relocate existing "Blueberry Ash" into proposed garden bed.

Communal area to allow for group gatherings/activities/social events.

Opportunity to have audio and visual facilities such as TV & stereo.

Main path

sand

Retain existing hedge along back wall.

Enhance existing planting with accent plants such as:
Cordyline 'Rubra'
Tradescantia spathacea
Agave attenuata
Macrozamia sp.

Relocate existing "Blueberry Ash" into proposed garden bed.

Sloping lawn.

Flat lawn.

secret
law

Feature tree such as:
"Weeping Cherry"

Recycled timber archway with scented climbers and wind charms.

Cobblestones in water to mediate crossover.

Textured groundcovers such as:
Stachys byzantine "Lamb's Ears"

Feat
such

Scen
Gai

Lawn nooks

Feature full length mosaic artwork.

Proposed new door garden entry.

Accent shrubs and groundcovers such as:
Tibouchina 'Jules' "Lesiandra"
Tradescantia sp.
Alternanthera sp.
Phormium Dwarf species "NZ Flax"
Echinacea purpurea "Purple Coneflower"

Feature cobblestone paving.

Ornamental groundcover planting to soften hard surfaces.

Timber batten screens for additional privacy.

Timber day bed to accommodate for 2-3 people.

Feature walls defining space, surface to be treated differently in different nooks with stone cladding, textured paint, object inlays, mosaic tiles etc.

Recycled timber pergola / arch placed along path to enhance experience.

Scented climbers over arch.

Varying carvings on exposed surfaces of posts to allow touch.

Custom made hanging objects varying in material and size to create different sounds such as hollow timber, copper, plastic. Option to be able to hit objects for interactive play.

Feature paving to vary from nook to nook to give each nook its own character.

Day bed nooks

Recycled timber pergola / arch

Ornamental objects for touch and sound.

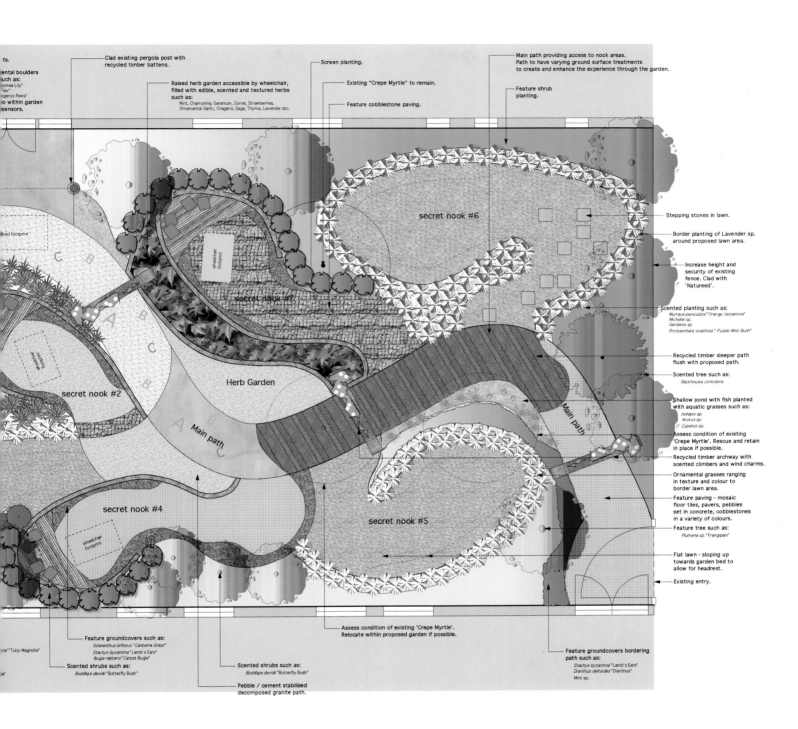

ts.

ental boulders
uch as:
ymea Lily"
lax"
garoo Paws"
o within garden
sensors.

Clad existing pergola post with
recycled timber battens.

Raised herb garden accessible by wheelchair,
filled with edible, scented and textured herbs
such as:
Mint, Chamomile, Geranium, Sorrel, Strawberries,
Ornamental Garlic, Oregano, Sage, Thyme, Lavender etc.

Screen planting.

Existing "Crepe Myrtle" to remain.

Feature cobblestone paving.

Main path providing access to nook areas.
Path to have varying ground surface treatments
to create and enhance the experience through the garden.

Feature shrub
planting.

secret nook #6

Stepping stones in lawn.

Border planting of Lavender sp.
around proposed lawn area.

Increase height and
security of existing
fence. Clad with
'Natureed'.

Scented planting such as:
Murraya paniculata "Orange Jessamine"
Michelia sp.
Gardenia sp.
Prostanthera ovalifolia " Purple Mint Bush"

Recycled timber sleeper path
flush with proposed path.

Scented tree such as:
Backhousia citriodora.

Shallow pond with fish planted
with aquatic grasses such as:
Isolepis sp.
Acorus sp.
Cyperus sp.

Assess condition of existing
'Crepe Myrtle'. Rescue and retain
in place if possible.

Recycled timber archway with
scented climbers and wind charms.

Ornamental grasses ranging
in texture and colour to
border lawn area.

Feature paving - mosaic
floor tiles, pavers, pebbles
set in concrete, cobblestones
in a variety of colours.

Feature tree such as:
Plumeria sp. "Frangipani"

Flat lawn - sloping up
towards garden bed to
allow for headrest.

Existing entry.

secret nook #7

Herb Garden

Main path

Main path

secret nook #2

secret nook #4

wheelchair
footprint

secret nook #5

bed footprint

Feature groundcovers such as:
Scleranthus biflorus "Canberra Grass"
Stachys byzantina "Lamb's Ears"
Ajuga reptans "Carpet Bugle"

Scented shrubs such as:
Buddleja davidii "Butterfly Bush"

Scented shrubs such as:
Buddleja davidii "Butterfly Bush"

Pebble / cement stabilised
decomposed granite path.

Assess condition of existing 'Crepe Myrtle'.
Relocate within proposed garden if possible.

Feature groundcovers bordering
path such as:
Stachys byzantina "Lamb's Ears"
Dianthus deltoides "Dianthus"
Mint sp.

PATIO
LANDSCAPE ARCHITECTURE
& DESIGN

(ABOVE) Water travels down the decorative mosaic wall and extends visually through the garden, allowing the children to safely interact with water.

(LEFT) Hidden nooks provide places to hide special treasures.

(FAR LEFT) A wind chime and wet-wall water feature introduces sound into the garden to serenade the senses.

(OPPOSITE) Shaded areas throughout the garden provide spaces for private- and quiet-time.

A NEW WAVE

Designed for the 2004 Pacific Flora World Garden Competition held in Shizuoka prefecture in Japan, this sculptural outdoor room combines natural and artificial materials finely crafted and rigorously engineered to put imaginations on high alert.

It's an elliptical deck encircled like an amphitheatre by terraced garden beds of concrete and rock, and cut off, like an island, by a reflection pond. A gentle ribbon of water spills over weirs in the garden beds into the pond, barely disrupting the stillness of the surface.

Access to the deck is only achieved via timber steppers floating just above the surface of the water. The main deck splits down the centre like a clam, revealing a pocket of Australian native violets (*Viola hederacea*) that suggest, perhaps, the secret entry to a hidden realm.

It took master boat-builders to hand-bend all the timber for the curved sections of decking to give the floor a sense of movement and unexpected visual illusions. The effect of the raised garden beds as they taper down towards the pond heightens the decks sense of shelter and seclusion.

Australian and New Zealand native plants included striking grass trees (*Xanthorrhoea* sp.), *Banksia integrifolia* and *Cordyline australis* as features across the top terraces. The lower terraces were massed with clumps of single species chosen for colour and texture, including *Cordyline* 'Red Star', kangaroo paw (*Anigozanthos flavidus*), *Carex hachijoensis* 'Evergold', the New Zealand flax *Phormium tenax* 'Dazzler' and *Grevillea* 'Poorinda Royal Mantle'.

With its vibrant contrasts of timber and stone, flowers and foliage, water and concrete, the space is alive with dynamic rhythms of colour, texture and form. The garden won awards for 'Excellence for Inspiration' and 'Design and Construction', and was viewed by more than 8 million people over its six-month lifespan from April to October 2004.

(LEFT) Hardwood steppers in the reflection pond are shaped like the shells of giant turtles. These are the only access point for the main deck.

(RIGHT) Seating for the courtyard runs along the base of the terraced walls. The gabion rock walls were filled with local stone. Along the highest rock walls, Australian native grass trees and *Cordyline australis* were planted as sentinels.

(OPPOSITE) Contrasting shapes and textures create dynamic tension in the built forms – rectangular rock-filled terraced walls and the sweeping curves of the deck where a 'split' in the middle reveals a seam of Australian native violets.

PERSONAL SANCTUARY

Gardens are our touchstone with the natural world. They connect with the rhythms of nature, which brings us closer to ourselves. In a busy secular world we increasingly bring symbols of harmony and goodwill into our gardens, which we use as a place to restore our sense of balance.

For this garden designed around a natural therapies centre within a busy shopping district, the aim was to create a series of very private spaces, that shut out the street activity and allowed those who were inside the centre to unwind.

In the first room, a life-size stone Buddha sits on a timber platform. Regardless of religion the meditating Buddha has come to symbolise inner peace, strength and harmony – even in the Western world. Each room is built using raw natural materials with refined detail. Frames for the partitioning screens are built in a similar style to the *Torii* – the iconic gateways to Shinto shrines in Japan that mark the entry to a sacred space. Nature-reed screens are fixed to these frames, offering privacy while allowing breezes and dappled light to penetrate. Dividing the ground plane are chunky timber sleepers and sandstone stepping stones set into white quartz pebbles.

Planted under the existing canopy of trees are the giant bird of paradise (*Strelitzia nicolai*) and cycads, the oyster plant (*Acanthus mollis*), with a spectacular spring flower spike can reach well over 1 metre, and the delicate flowering groundcover *Ajuga reptans* – both of these thicken in time. These plants were chosen for lush, generous leaves and flowers to promote an atmosphere of vitality and to provide surprises as the seasons change.

Aside from the Buddha, two conical metal bowls on beds of black pebbles are quiet symbols of reflection. Water spills gently over the sides of the bowls with the most soothing trickling sound, while the surrounding sky and trees are reflected in the surface like a mirror.

SENSORY
IN FOCUS

Lift the spirits, excite the imagination,

let the mind wander. Tap into creative energy.

Walk among the trees. Speak to the senses:

touch, sight, smell, sound – with water, wind,

flowers and foliage. Use natural materials

with a twist. Playfulness equals vitality.

Reconnect with nature –

nature heals.

UND OBJECTS INTO FUNCTIONAL OBJECTS

STATUES

BRIDGES, STREAMS, LAKES AND PONDS

SCULPTURE ART

MATERIALS AND DESIGN ELEMENTS

CHARACTER AND AGED OBJECTS

MIRRORS

FOUND OBJECTS INTO ART

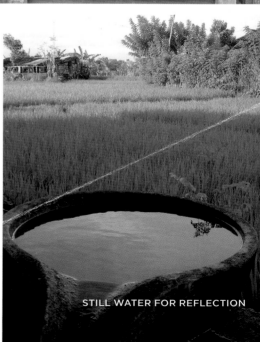
STILL WATER FOR REFLECTION

🌿 *Acacia elata* CEDAR WATTLE

🌿 *Eucalyptus* 'Summer Beauty' SUMMER BEAUTY GUM

☙🌿 *Melaleuca quinquenery*
BROAD-LEAFED PAPERBAR

☙ ✿ *Lavandula stoechas* ITALIAN LAVENDER

SENSORY PLANTS

✿ SMELL

☙ TOUCH

🌿 SIGHT & BIRD ATTRACTING

☙ *Stachys byzantina* LAMBS' EAR

✿ *Gardenia augusta* GARDENIA

🌿 *Callistemon viminalis* 'Little John'
LITTLE JOHN BOTTLEBRUSH

✿ *Backhousia citriodo*
LEMON-SCENTED MYRT

✿ *Citrus* cv CITRUS

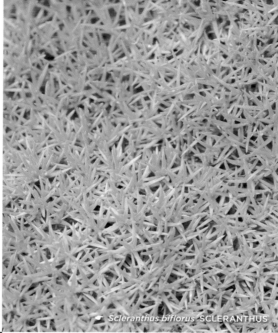

🍃 *Scleranthus biflorus* 'SCLERANTHUS'

✿ *Stephanotis floribunda* MADAGASCAR JASMINE

🍃 *Kalanchoe tomentosa* PANDA PLANT

🍃 MOSS

✿ *Citrus limon* LEMON

✿ *Thelychiton speciosus* ROCK ORCHID

🍃 *Banksia ericifolia* HEATH BANKSIA

✿ *Jasminum sambac* 'Grand Duke of Tuscany'
GRAND DUKE OF TUSCANY JASMINE

new directions

THE NATURAL LANDSCAPE HAS BECOME AUSTRALIA'S MOST POWERFUL CULTURAL SYMBOL. NEARLY EVERY ADVERTISEMENT FOR TOURISM CELEBRATES OUR ENVIRONMENT WITH MAGNIFICENT PANORAMIC VISTAS OF THE LANDSCAPE – FROM THE RED CENTRE TO THE BARRIER REEF, FROM LUSH RAINFORESTS TO GOLDEN BEACHES.

It's what people from all over the world come here to experience. And it's what we as Australians are finally starting to appreciate.

Our country is blessed with great climatic diversity, but up until quite recently our gardening ideals were those imported by our founders, and largely inappropriate for our conditions. In the 1940s, it was the influential landscape designer Edna Walling who said that Australia should look to Spain and Italy for gardening inspiration, not England. Walling's philosophy was not simply to copy from Mediterranean countries, but to start appreciating our own unique indigenous flora and weave it into our gardens. In 1952 she published a book called *The Australian Roadside*, to encourage Australians to see the beauty of our native species and stop the indiscriminate clearing of natural vegetation. She urged readers to 'not continue to view the roadside plants as so much "scrub" but as the very interesting, fitting and invaluable plants they really are'. She was all the more persuasive because although Walling was heavily influenced by the British style when she began designing gardens in 1920, the Australian landscape won her over. She began to use more and more natives, incorporating them into the planting schemes along with exotics to create more natural-style landscaping that united the Australian house with its garden. She is widely regarded as the designer who bridged the gap between our old-world landscaping and the new.

Being a young country, we've always borrowed and adapted ideas from other cultures and this has sometimes seen us easily seduced by exotic plants and styles. After our forays with tropical gardens overflowing with tree ferns, palms, ponds and orchids, came the parterre garden with its clipped box hedges, or worse, the 'Leighton Green' cypress – you got a few good years from these overgrown monsters before you had to rip them out. Next there was the Mediterranean phase – all Tuscany and terracotta-potted geraniums, lavender and citrus. Then the minimalist phase arrived – with Modernist-Zen reflection ponds replacing natural pools, and planting reduced to an architectural minimum. For the last few years, succulents have ruled because they are perfectly at home in our climate, they're almost indestructible when it comes to neglect, and they have a beautiful architectural quality to them which makes them ideal for people whose garden is a balcony. What's not to love?

Thankfully, after all this experimenting we're developing a gardening language of our own and native plants are very much a part of it. We're using them in interesting ways more suited to our conditions, which is making people look at natives in a new light. It's a trend that's happening worldwide and with good reason. Gardens are not always about impressing our architecture on their natural forms. Intelligent gardening is about choosing plants that can deliver the structure, the intimacy, the colour, the texture, the shapes and the shelter that we need. As weather patterns change under the influence of global warming, the environment is forcing us to stop and think about the effects of how we build, farm and garden. In Australia, it's predicted that rainfall will further decrease over much of the country and bushfires are likely to increase. Water is already at a premium. If a garden is to survive, and thrive, we should see it as an investment, just as we see our houses. Because it's a living, growing landscape, we should invest in suitable plants for the conditions, improvements to the soil where necessary, and, critically, how we use the water. The cool green lawn, once an icon of the great Australian dream home, has become something of a nightmare in today's climate of drought. Long out of step with the tough sclerophyll landscape that wraps around much of Australia, they've become a luxury that most simply can't afford.

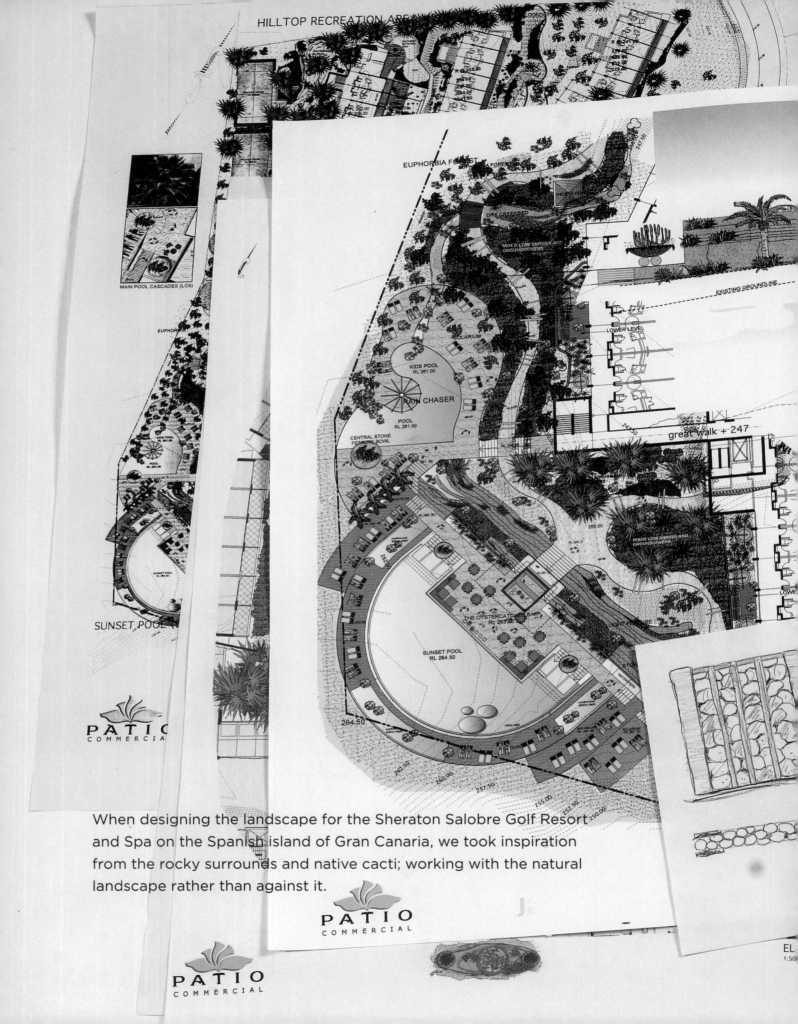

When designing the landscape for the Sheraton Salobre Golf Resort and Spa on the Spanish island of Gran Canaria, we took inspiration from the rocky surrounds and native cacti; working with the natural landscape rather than against it.

SUITE POOL - LO7

LEGEND
STONE PAVED AREAS
SOLARIUM AREA

COURTYARD

POOL

...TEL
...CANARIA

SPA

SALOBRE
THE OTHERSIDE/TONEA BAR
SUNSET POOL

SUNSET POOL BEYOND

260.27

SHERATON SALOBRE GOLF & SPA HOTEL — GRAN CANARIA

SUNSET BAR
RL 263.50

STONE WALL WITH SOLOBRE
INSIGNIA

SUNSET POOL
TW 264.50

INFORMAL STONE STEPS

SOLARIUM

SPILL OVER AND RESERVOIR

METAL BOLT INTO ROCK

STAINLESS WIRE
WATER URN

3 2800mm TIMBER
HARDWOOD POSTS
WITH UPLIGHTS.

LOW PLANTING.

REAR WALL SKETCH.

LIGHT

EXCAVATED LOOSE PEBBLE

STONE SLAB CONTOURED
INFORMAL STEPS

SALOBRE

SUNSET POOL LO8

SCALE 1:200   JOB No.03-066   DECEMBER 2003

ENTRY GARDEN

SALOBRE

ENTRY AND AERIAL GARDEN LO2

SCALE 1:200   JOB No.03-066   DECEMBER 2003

OPEN HOUSE

This concept gives an entirely new meaning to the phrase 'bringing the outside in'. Two exterior walls of the house are designed as vertically pivoting gardens, allowing the owner to rotate the walls – both for a change of garden scenery indoors and to maintain a healthy garden by providing the required amount of sunlight to each side of the wall. This design also allows the walls to be kept half-open so that the house not only becomes part of the garden, but is flooded with fresh air, sunshine and views of the landscape beyond...

Garden design by Jamie Durie. Illustration by Alex Augustyn.

ROTATING WALLS
(TEXTURED CLADDING)

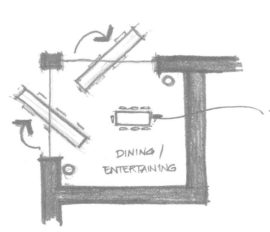

PLAN SKETCH

DINING /
ENTERTAINING

DINING | ENTERTAIN

PLANTERS

AREA

Traditional doors that became exterior walls were in my mind after seeing these gates.

Local grasses have become an attractive alternative to lawn as landscape designers use them in architectural ways. In New Zealand, landscape designer Ted Smyth mixes natives with exotics to striking effect, particularly in his coastal gardens that take a lashing from the weather. He'll mass together grasses of different heights as an understorey or groundcover with a strong feature plant rising from it – for instance the dragon tree (Dracaena draco), a slow grower from the Canary Islands that reaches around 9 metres, with a crown of stiff, straplike leaves. For other gardens he'll stick to natives only, where it's appropriate to the site, such as those near sensitive native forest. For Smyth it's about using native plants to express a garden's 'sense of place' within the wider landscape.

In Australia, architect Glenn Murcutt has encouraged us to celebrate a 'sense of place' since the late 1960s with his quintessentially Australian houses, famous for their curves and corrugated steel cladding. He pioneered the idea of using simple, honest building materials from rural Australia in a refined way that suits urban aesthetics and sits in harmony with nature. What you notice about his houses, in rural or remote settings, is that they have virtually no built landscaping around them. Instead, they frame the surrounding natural landscape through walls of glass going up to skillion roofs, making it the focus of the interior. You literally feel like you're living in the landscape and in this way he is paying homage to the natural landscape.

Since Australia was settled, nearly a million square kilometres of native forest and bush, mallee, heath and grassland have been cleared, mostly for agriculture or timber production. Fragile ecosystems have been lost and the door has been opened to the spread of invasive plant species introduced from overseas. The way forward requires greater care with our land practices, and ingenuity in repairing the damage.

Weathered materials like rusted steel compliment the harsh landscape. In this environment, the architecture is amplified.

While designing a garden last year in Wagga Wagga, western New South Wales, the PATIO team encountered first-hand the problem of salination. This is where over-irrigation had caused the water table to rise, bringing salt to the topsoil and killing the plants. This usually occurs in rural areas, but as old farming estates are carved up into new housing estates, home-owners inherit the problem. To make the garden viable we removed a lot of the salt-laden soil, replacing it with fresh soil and organic matter, and used a palette of salt- and drought-hardy plants; we found 75 that were tolerant to both, most of them indigenous to the region. For irrigation we built underground lines at root level for controlled release of water only where it's needed so it doesn't add to the problem, and it's fed from rainwater tanks.

Beyond our own backyards, more people around the country are getting involved at the grass-roots level to help repair and protect the environment. This is one of my greatest passions, and it's a privilege to have worked with Planet Ark for the past 12 years. Since 1996, more than 9 million native trees and shrubs have been planted around Australia through its National Tree Day program. In 2005 I joined other Planet Ark ambassadors and more than 350,000 volunteers in planting 1.5 million native plants at 4,000 locations around Australia. In 2006 our national campaign got schools involved, and encouraged a competitive team spirit from state to state in towns around the country to see how many trees each school and each town planted on the day. It was a fantastic community-building project. If you can mix the environment and kids together now and teach them what we know about how to fix the damage and prevent it happening again, what an amazing planet we're going to have when they're older. I think the commitment of people to these projects says a lot about our future. What could be more positive than bringing people and plants together?

RESIDENCE

GLASS WALLS TO ROOMS

DIFFERENT GARDEN TYPES TO SUIT VARIED ASPECT

With this design I really wanted to bring the outside in and let every room experience a different landscape. The roof also becomes an inspirational place to be – every inch of the vertical and horizontal space is kissed by nature!

Garden design by Jamie Durie. Illustration by Alex Augustyn.

The simple shape of a leaf inspired this concept.

LEGEND

1 stairs
2 porch
3 tatami room
4 hibachi
5 day-bed
6 stairs
7 covered walkway
8 w.c.
9 garden storage
10 pergola walkway
11 buré
12 banquette
13 pond garden
14 "living" room
15 conservatory
16 palm garden
17 kitchen
18 dining room above (glass louvre ceiling)
19 grotto
20 outdoor room
21 pool
22 meditation deck
23 lava shack
24 charles lawn
25 bbq

'Is it a house or a garden Wally?
The dream is the *in between...* '

While I love doing my bit for the environment and helping others with their dream gardens, I've also been dreaming of my own space for some time. And it's starting to take shape. I live in an old house on the northern beaches of Sydney, and have been working on plans to build my dream home.

The architect I'm working with is Walter Barda, who's also an artist, and I think by now a friend. He has patiently indulged me and listened to all the wild tangents I tend to go off on when I'm passionate about an idea. I think some of our ideas about building houses and landscapes are similar. I like his aesthetic – it's refined yet primitive. Wally says, 'architecture is all about caves and trees' which sounds like fun to me. He says a home should be a continuum from inside to out. His buildings have a muscular, sculptural form to shelter you from the elements, with surprises and areas that get you among the treetops. I like the sound of that too.

I've always wanted a house with no walls. Like a Balinese compound where the perimeter is lockable, but the house itself is open. Obviously in Sydney you have to adjust your expectations a little and work out the logistics. It's been two years in the making and we are still polishing the design. At the moment it exists only on paper and in mine and Wally's minds, but this is how I explain it. Once you step inside the main gate, you'll never really know if you're inside or out. All those boundaries will be blurred. I want the landscaping to feel like a lounge room and the whole interior to feel like it's part of the garden. The living area will have a huge glass dome over the top of it, like a terrarium. Under it will be trees and palms and sofas and tables, and a wall of water beside the dining room. The different rooms and sections will be separated by landscape features and changes in the levels, not walls – there won't really be any... and that's my idea of paradise.

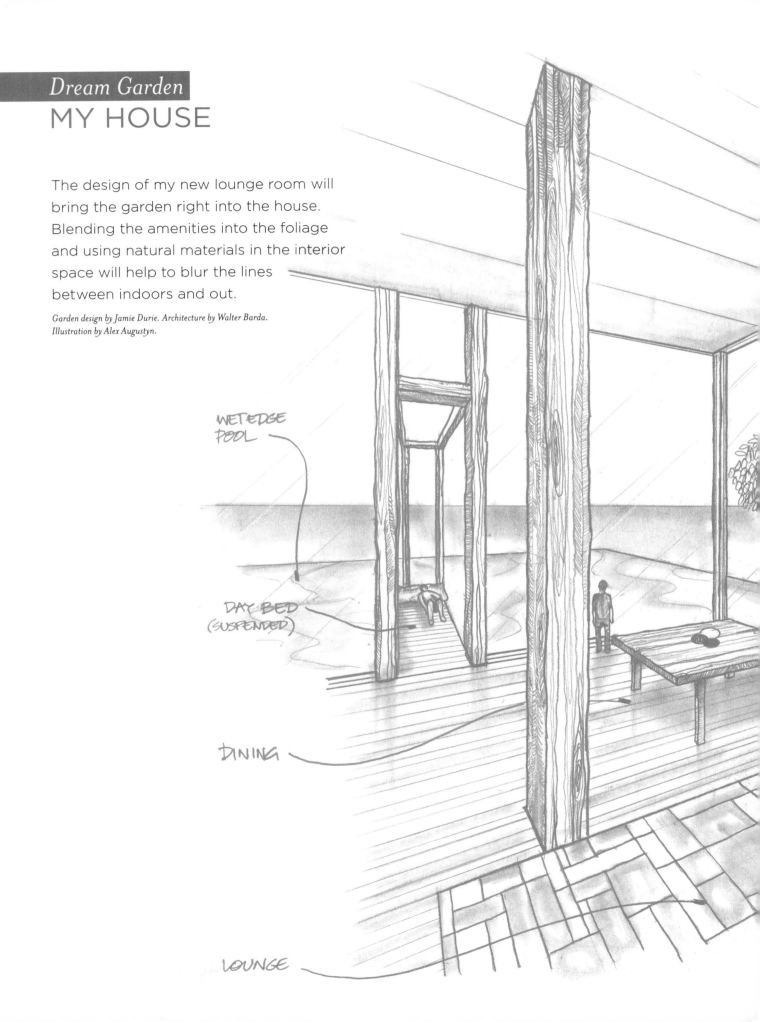

MY HOUSE

The design of my new lounge room will
bring the garden right into the house.
Blending the amenities into the foliage
and using natural materials in the interior
space will help to blur the lines
between indoors and out.

Garden design by Jamie Durie. Architecture by Walter Barda.
Illustration by Alex Augustyn.

WET EDGE
POOL

DAY BED
(SUSPENDED)

DINING

LOUNGE

OPEN ATRIUM & GARDEN

A simple harmonious union between indoors and out provided the inspiration for this design.

TIMBER & STONE FLOORING

'Looking back over my personal travel pics, I've realised that DESIGN REALLY IS IN THE DETAIL and that's why it's so important to record every single piece of this visual kaleidescope – they're like fertiliser for creativity.'

'Architectural inspiration doesn't just come from built form
— IT'S ALL AROUND US.'

'Extreme landscapes have always inspired me. Understanding each plans broad CAPABILITY AND RESILIENCE provides you with an endless scope.'

'The trick is to be BRAVE AND INNOVATIVE in order to procure the idea and convert it into a feasable design that also has function.'

'Nothing moves me more than nature itself...

the best ideas come naturally.

BE INSPIRED.'